A GOC TOMORROW

By the same author

Novels
The River Running By
The Raging of the Sea
The Believer
Armada
The Fighting Spirit
The Crying of the Wind
Jannaway's Mutiny

Philosophy
Basic Flying Instruction

A GOOD BOY TOMORROW

◆

Memoirs of a Fundamentalist Upbringing

Charles Gidley Wheeler

iUniverse, Inc.
New York Lincoln Shanghai

A GOOD BOY TOMORROW
Memoirs of a Fundamentalist Upbringing

Copyright © 2007 by Charles Gidley Wheeler

All rights reserved. No part of this book may be used or reproduced by any means, graphic, electronic, or mechanical, including photocopying, recording, taping or by any information storage retrieval system without the written permission of the publisher except in the case of brief quotations embodied in critical articles and reviews.

iUniverse books may be ordered through booksellers or by contacting:

iUniverse
2021 Pine Lake Road, Suite 100
Lincoln, NE 68512
www.iuniverse.com
1-800-Authors (1-800-288-4677)

The views expressed in this work are solely those of the author and do not necessarily reflect the views of the publisher, and the publisher hereby disclaims any responsibility for them.

ISBN: 978-0-595-43685-9 (pbk)
ISBN: 978-0-595-88018-8 (ebk)

Printed in the United States of America

Note

It is just a hundred years since Edmund Gosse's classic autobiography *Father and Son* was first published. Although when I read it thirty years ago I saw a close similarity between Gosse's account of his upbringing among the Plymouth Brethren and my own childhood among the Open Brethren, I assumed that such exclusive fundamentalism was a thing of the past.

Of course, I was wrong. Evangelical sects are flourishing in the USA, Britain, and Europe, and there can be no doubt that thousands of children are still being taught, from their earliest years, that they are stained with original sin, that the end of the world is nigh and that unless they accept Christ as their Savior they will suffer eternal punishment in hell. Speaking from my own experience, I believe that this sort of religious indoctrination is not only psychologically damaging, but that it plays a significant part in rendering children vulnerable to sexual abuse at the hands of those in authority.

It is for people who have been damaged by an over-strict religious upbringing that I have written this book. Even if it helps only one person to shed their burden of religious anxiety, my work will not have been in vain.

C.G.W.

1

My grandfather, Walter Gidley Wheeler, was a member of the exclusive sect of Plymouth Brethren, and a leading light in the assembly of saints at Cholmeley Hall in Highgate. He was the owner of a printing and publishing business on Paternoster Row close to St. Paul's Cathedral, and married to Florence Burbridge, a small person with prominent front teeth and an unpredictable temper. They were comfortably off and lived at Enfield on the outskirts of London.

Walter died of pneumonia in 1914 at the age of fifty-two, leaving Florence with three children: May, James, and Walter. These three were known as Maisie, Jim, and Wally, later shortened to Wal.

James had set his heart on going into the Navy, but he contracted measles while studying for the entrance examination for Dartmouth Naval College, with the result that he failed the eyesight test and in 1917 went into the army instead. At Sandhurst, he proved himself to be an outstanding horseman. He was commissioned into the Fifth Irish Lancers; and to the immense relief of his mother he was posted abroad for service in India rather than to the trenches in France. He was every inch a cavalry officer and liked by the men it was his privilege to command. But after the war his widowed mother, who signed herself "Mother Hen" in her weekly letters to him, began pressurizing him to resign his commission and return home to help her look after Wal, who was slightly disabled.

James was reluctant to comply with his mother's wishes. Following a mutiny in 1919, the Fifth Irish Lancers was disbanded and he was now commissioned in the First Royal Dragoon Guards, which considered itself to be at the top of the pecking order in the British Army. But Mother Hen was not easily thwarted. She stopped his allowance, rendering him unable to pay the high mess and tailor's bills of a cavalry officer, and forcing him to resign his commission and end a promising military career.

He left the army in 1924 and returned home. He had had seven years of polo and gin slings. Now it was time to help Wal with his poultry farm, which within a few months proved to be an unmitigated disaster.

Soon after his return from India, in the summer of 1924, James spent a brief bucket-and-spade holiday in darkest Devon with his cousins the Prettyjohns. Molly Prettyjohn, an attractive, dark-haired girl who later did time for kleptomania, was thirteen at the time and had a crush on James, which turned into a lifelong infatuation after he saved her from drowning:

> My dearest Wheeler I,
>
> I am writing to thank you so much for coming in so sportingly to fish me out at Lanacombe. I could not thank you properly when you were down here, because you always laughed it off. I may not have seemed very grateful. But truth to tell I couldn't think what to say. It was <u>ripping</u> of you. I miss you awfully. You have left your boot brush. I will send it on. Hilda goes tomorrow. Betty has got CHICKEN POX so we shall be cooped up here for 3 weeks. Isn't it rotten luck? Betty has 50 spots on her face alone. I have not seen her since she developed it. Twopence and Poodles send their love also Mum Dad & Betty.
> With tons of love,
> Your affectionate cousin
> Molly.

When Mother Hen wasn't looking, James took up with the fast set. He had ambitions as a playwright and had an affair with an actress, for whom he wrote a stage play that was never produced. But after a while, he was brought to heel and was once more at Mother Hen's side (Wal was on the other) at the Sunday Morning Meeting at Cholmeley Hall for the breaking of bread. It was here that he first set eyes on Joyce Marks.

Joyce, whose name was borrowed by Edmund Gosse to protect the privacy of one of the characters in his autobiography *Father and Son*, was born in Rutherford, New Jersey on August 26, 1900. She was the younger of two girls. Her father, Robert Chapman Marks, was an insurance broker. Her mother was Laura Wilmot and her grandfather was the owner of the steam shipping line Burgess & Co, whose ships sailed from Bristol. When Joyce was two years old, her parents' marriage broke up and Laura took her two daughters back to Britain to stay with her parents at Mumbles on the Gower Coast of Glamorganshire in The Croft, a mansion set in its own grounds that later became the home of the first Labor British Prime Minister, Ramsay MacDonald.

Within a few years of her return to Wales, Laura contracted rheumatoid arthritis and became bedridden. One of Joyce's most vivid childhood memories was of hearing her mother coughing, and rushing upstairs to help her up into a sitting position to prevent her from choking.

When Laura died in 1911 at the age of forty-one, Joyce stayed on with her grandparents at the Croft; but when she was seventeen Mr. Gold, the owner of a jewelry shop in Swansea, lured her to his house on a false pretext and attempted to have his wicked way with her. She fled with her virtue intact but her trust in the opposite sex badly affected, and was sent to London to be out of harm's way. She worked at the Islington Medical Mission among the slum children of London's East End and later trained as a nurse at University College Hospital on Gower Street.

Joyce was also a "Peeb," as the lighter hearted members of the Plymouth Brethren referred to themselves, and one Sunday after the breaking of bread at Cholmeley Hall, Mrs. Wheeler invited her to tea. Her meeting with James, whom she addressed as JG in her letters, marked the beginning of a seven year courtship during which she fled from him twice—first to New Zealand, and later to Northern Rhodesia, where her sister Ethelwyn and her husband Dr. ffolliott Fisher ran a hospital and Christian mission.

After two years on the mission station Joyce returned to Britain where, after many letters, meetings and afternoon teas—as well as quite a few changes of mind on her part—she and JG were finally married in 1931.

The wedding reception was held at the house of their friend and benefactor Mrs. Boake. Joyce looked lovely in a demure wedding dress with veil, and James, in top hat, tails, and spats, looked dashing with his neatly clipped military mustache, his twinkling smile, and his straight-backed, cavalry officer's bearing. The only slight hitch was the receipt of a telegram addressed to Joyce. It was from her childhood sweetheart, Billy, and read, DISREGARD LETTER. When Billy's letter eventually arrived from Australia, it contained a proposal of marriage. Billy later became the Bishop of Sydney.

By this time, Mother Hen had spent much of the fortune inherited from her late husband on doctors' bills, lunches out, and trips into town to visit her dressmaker. So it was with Joyce's small amount of capital that the newly wedded couple bought 67 Brent Way, a three bedroom terraced house in Finchley, north London.

After working as a publisher for some years, JG joined a firm in the docklands of east London, where he had part ownership of a wharf on the Thames. Joyce had a miscarriage in 1932, but in March 1933, Susan arrived. She was followed three years later by Janice, who was followed two years after that, on August 21, 1938, by yours sincerely, who reportedly bawled his head off for the first six months of his life.

2

As the storm clouds gathered in the summer of 1939, James took steps to move the family to safety. The house at 67 Brent Way was put up for rent, and the family removed to temporary lodgings with Joyce's aunt in Mumbles. Joyce and Jim spent three days together, walking on the cliffs and treasuring their last moments before JG went to London to volunteer for service in the Army.

Within a few weeks of war being declared, he was back in uniform and working in the War Office on the staff of the Military Secretary with responsibility for the selection of senior officers for key posts in the British Expeditionary Force. This was the beginning of nearly eight years of separation, during which JG and JM were together for a total of little more than three weeks.

Seeing an opportunity to work with ships, JG secured an appointment to the Royal Engineers with the task of forming and manning the Inland Water Transport Division. In March 1940, he took command of No. 12 Dock Section and moved to France, where he was involved in unloading cargo ships carrying materials for the extension of the Maginot Line.

A month later, his Section was sent to Douai. Here, he was comfortably billeted in a *gentilhommière* on the outskirts of the town by the canal. As spring sprung and the "phony war" continued, life was pleasant. The canal barges came steadily up from Amiens, were emptied of sand and cement, and sent back down the canal for more. For a few weeks, while Hitler's generals completed their preparations for the invasion of Belgium and France, life was quite agreeable, and JG found time to write home to Joyce:

>   No. 12 Docks Section R.E.
>   I Corps B.E.F.
>   6-5-40
>
> My love, my sweet,
>
> I'm sitting up in bed (11.25 p.m.) in the most beautiful billet <u>ever</u> allotted to a British Officer. My hostess is the French equivalent of Auntie Boake, but with that superlative touch of "Grande Dame" that makes you forget that ever the money was <u>made</u>, or that ever a favour were being bestowed. She puts Eau de Cologne on my

marble-topped washing basin, and garden violets at my bedside. My room is high, with two full-length windows; a wardrobe with large, authentic Vauxhall mirror; an immense linen press, which would comfortably hold all the clothes I have ever possessed, and a BED. I really hope that, when this bloodiest of all bloodless wars is ended, you and I will be able to come here and sleep in this very bed, and then I could take you round and show you where I did some of the enthralling things I've been doing. And Madame would be enchanted to look through new snaps of the kids, and tell me again how proud and happy I should be over our joint achievement!

That means I have the birthday letter and the Polyfoto pictures of Jan & Charles and of J, C and S. They're marvellous. They live in the wallet, with various other treasures, and I'm afraid I produce them pretty well everywhere as a means of exciting the enthusiasm of the French. One really good thing about these people is that they do genuinely worship children, and a good mother is to them almost as sacred as Notre Dame de Quelque Part.

My own precious One, I <u>know</u> there must be letters piling up for me, and that they will, one day, arrive. But meanwhile I just carry about your letter saying you hadn't heard from me, and long to know that your mind is at rest. Now, I do hope things will run more smoothly, and that you will get a letter at least <u>once</u> a week. When secrecy is over, I will tell you all about it. The great thing now is to be really sure that you will get this in a day or two.

You do realize that for the time being I have missed my leave, don't you? Just before all this happened, when I was due to go, young C. got news that his child was much worse, and that they wanted to operate immediately. Of course, I thought I could chop my leave with his, and come 10 days later. He went about looking like a tortured ghost, and I simply hadn't the gall to hold him back. Then the leave hold-up came, and after that, this. And now I must start up all over again, and find out when my turn will come. I pray every day that it won't be far off.

It's impossible to tell you much just now. I've got the most wonderful crowd of boys, who are just falling over themselves with enthusiasm, and I feel almost as I used to do when I was a terrific success as a junior cavalry subaltern with two years' staff experience. It's almost incredible, the way I have <u>slid</u> through to the kind of job I was looking for.

My One, you're having the foul end of this bloody war, with all the worries, and no feeling of <u>getting</u> anywhere. But, my own treasure, your letters and the continuity of HOME they give to me are the only counterbalance I have against ALL THIS 'ERE. In this bed, I sleep on <u>your</u> side, and when I wake up in the morning, I always feel guilty.

Good-night, beloved. I'm not so faint and far away, but waiting and longing for you, trying for the earliest chance to be with me.

Kiss me.
All your JG

Early one sunny morning five days after JG sat up in bed and wrote his letter, a German bomber hammered overhead and dropped the first stick of bombs on Douai. It was May 10, 1940. The invasion of France and the Low Countries had begun.

No. 12 Dock Section consisted of one lorry and forty lightly armed men. On the outbreak of the blitzkrieg, JG was ordered to take them back to Boulogne for evacuation and return to England. Quite a lot of other people had similar ideas and the order, like so many orders at that time, was more easily given than obeyed. The main roads were blocked with refugees; Stukas were dive-bombing at will; water was in short supply, and the German Grossdeutschland regiment, having broken through at Saumur, was advancing rapidly to Abbeville on the coast.

The retreat to Boulogne could only be made in safety by avoiding contact with the enemy. JG was fluent in French and good at map reading. He took his section into the country lanes, camouflaged the vehicles, and trained the men to dive for cover at the sound of approaching aircraft. It was touch and go whether the section would make it back to Boulogne and at one stage he gathered his men together and told them that if anyone felt that he would have a better chance of survival by proceeding on his own, he was free to leave and would not be charged with desertion. No one took that option, and the section arrived without loss or injury at a deserted farmhouse on the outskirts of Boulogne—very hot, very tired, and extremely thirsty. In the farmhouse kitchen were a dozen or so bottles of lemonade, which were immediately uncorked by the sappers with whoops of joy; but the whoops turned to exclamations of revulsion: the bottles contained not lemonade, but olive oil.

JG reported his arrival to Lieutenant General Brownrigg's headquarters at Wimereux. Brownrigg informed him that, in the absence of any other fighting troops, No. 12 Dock Section was to form the center section defense of the Boulogne perimeter against the advancing spearhead of the German army—the 20th Panzer Division under the command of General Guderian, the architect of blitzkrieg.

JG returned to his section and proceeded to put his orders into effect as best he could. He commandeered vehicles and overturned them in the approach roads to the town. He felled trees across the country lanes, spread out his forty men in groups of four or five, and armed them with as many things that went bang as he could lay his hands on.

In due course, the Panzers rolled up and a night engagement began. Perhaps the tank commanders would have pressed their attack home with more determination had they known that they were up against forty non-fighting troops under the command of an ex-cavalry lieutenant who called his parent Mother Hen. Whatever the case, the cockney heroes of No. 12 Dock Section held out against the spearhead of Hitler's blitzkrieg for the best part of forty-eight hours when, mercifully, they were reinforced by the arrival of the Irish Guards, with whom JG and his section remained in action, being forced back by the overwhelming firepower of Guderian's tanks and Goering's Luftwaffe.

The Germans pushed quickly ahead and invested the town of Boulogne. The tanks took up positions in the approach roads to the port and the machine gunners in the top floor apartments overlooking the port, from where they fired down on anything that moved.

When the Irish Guards and No.12 Dock Section had retreated to the cover of the warehouses and repair sheds of the port, it was discovered that a wallet of signal codes had been left in a schoolroom that had been used as a temporary headquarters and was now behind enemy lines. This was a job for the cavalry, so JG jumped on a motorbike and rode hell-for-leather back into the town, dodging the German tanks, and back to the schoolroom, where he grabbed the wallet and rode back down the hill to rejoin his comrades in arms—a little sweaty, but otherwise unhurt.

Boulogne was by now awash with ill-disciplined non-fighting troops being evacuated, under machine gun fire and dive-bombing, a thousand at a time by destroyers of the Royal Navy. JG was evacuated on the last destroyer to leave the port, HMS *Vimiera*, on May 30. He and every single one of the men of No. 12 Dock Section returned to England in safety.

After the evacuation of Dunkirk, there were good grounds for the belief that Hitler would immediately press ahead with the invasion of Britain, and urgent action was taken to set up defenses on the Kent coast.

Promoted to captain and awarded the oak leaf insignia of a Mention in Dispatches for his part in the defense of Boulogne, JG was involved in setting up coastal defenses and training the first companies of the Home Guard—dramatized by David Croft in his classic television comedy series *Dad's Army*. Sixty years later, my wife and I met David Croft and his wife Ann, who have a house a few miles from ours in Portugal, and we became friends.

By the autumn of 1940, the threat of a German invasion had receded. Intelligence reports now indicated that Hitler planned to land paratroopers and fifth columnists in the Lake District of Westmorland and Cumberland. To counter this threat, JG was appointed in command of a unit whose mission was to set up lake defenses in northern England. He took up his headquarters at Windermere in the Royal Hotel and as soon as he was established there, he sent for Joyce and the three children, Susan, Jan, and Charles.

3

I was two years old when we moved north from Mumbles to the Lake District. For the first few months, my mother and sisters stayed in lodgings on the east side of Lake Windermere, while I was left with Phyllis, my nurse, in lodgings on the other side at Hawkshead. Being thus separated from my parents at so early an age may explain the sense of solitary independence that I have had as long as I can remember. It is a feeling that is encapsulated in the words of *The Miller's Song*, which as a little boy I sometimes sang, self-consciously drowning in tears of self-pity:

> I care for nobody, no, not I,
> Since nobody cares for me.

After a few months, my mother and sisters moved across to Hawkshead. Soon afterwards, my father was posted away, and we moved back to the east side of Lake Windermere, where we lived in various lodgings. Of these I remember three: the Hutch, a converted railway carriage that stood in the grounds of a house whose garden ran down to the water's edge, Beckside Cottage, which is a few miles from Bowness, and a log cabin in a forest on Tower Hill, which was so remote you could shout at the top of your voice on a quiet night and only the owls would hear.

While war raged in Europe, my slow awakening took place in idyllic surroundings of beauty and peace. My earliest memory is of sitting on my mother's knee while she clapped my hands together and sang:

> Clap hands 'til Daddy comes home,
> Daddy's got money but Mummy's got none,
> Clap hands 'til Daddy comes home …

The Langdale Pikes, which my mother used to paint in watercolors, stood blue in the northern distance. Forests of spruce marched up the hills on the other side of the lake, putting on their best green in the spring and turning teddy-bear gold in the autumn.

Behind Beckside Cottage was a field with a tree in it that I couldn't climb, but my sisters could. Beyond that were the ever wakeful fells, where the sheep bleated and the curlews cried and, on a summer's day, the larks rose high overhead.

Three of the teachers at Blackwell House School, where I started soon after my fifth birthday, lodged with us at Beckside Cottage. Their names, appropriately enough for a sheep farming district, were Miss Penn, Miss Herd, and Miss Booth. Miss Booth was sensual and a little fiery. Miss Herd was the epitome of a village schoolteacher: kind, patient, fair, and, as far as I was concerned, omniscient. Miss Penn was not entirely one of us, or at least, we were not quite one of her lot. She was a bit classy. She hummed and whispered to herself every night while practicing eurhythmics before going to bed.

Miss Murphy, the head mistress, was an eccentric Irish lady. She had a huge doll called Gloriana, which was the school mascot. Each year at Christmas, Gloriana had a birthday party at which some spectacle took place. Miss Murphy would dress up as Old Mother Hubbard or Mother Goose or The Old Woman Who Lived in a Shoe, and Gloriana would make a carefully staged, and usually dramatic, entrance. The most ambitious of these productions was an enactment of Little Miss Muffet, in which an extremely large and hairy spider came zooming down on a pulley from the rafters and sat down beside Gloriana (alias Miss Muffet)—though she was not, however, frightened away. Years later, when Margaret Thatcher became prime minister, her arrival at the annual Conservative party conference never failed to remind me of Gloriana's birthday parties at Blackwell House.

Miss Murphy always wore brown: a brown tweed jacket with a brown skirt, thick, baggy brown stockings, and extremely sensible brown brogues. She was a formidable woman whose unwavering self-confidence enabled her to make what she wanted to happen, happen. One particularly cold winter when Lake Windermere almost froze over, she decided that the whole school should learn to skate—not on the lake, but on an ice rink of her own making. She begged and borrowed skates from far and wide, organized a bucket chain from the kitchen tap to the circular driveway in front of the school, and within the space of an hour, the school had its own circular ice rink. On this, one morning, I learnt to skate and was so thoroughly bitten by the bug that I completely exhausted myself and had to be carried off the rink.

One morning during the Easter holidays, I was sent round to the school with a message to deliver to Miss Murphy. When I arrived, although the front doors were wide open, there seemed to be no one about. Hearing muffled noises from on high, I went up the broad staircase, and on, up narrower flights to the top floor, where I was confronted by the sight of my headmistress coming backwards down a ladder from the roof in a pair of voluminous flesh-pink knickers, a handkerchief worn highwayman style round her mouth and nose, and a pair of woolen underpants on her head. She had been cleaning out the main cistern. "Messy job," she observed to herself. "Yes, Charles? What is it, dear?"

Miss Murphy's teaching methods at Blackwell house were unhindered by government guidelines or targets. R-a-t spelt "rat" and if you put an "e" on the end, the "e" picked up the telephone to the "a" and told it to be a long "a" rather than a short one. More difficult spellings were learnt by marching home while reciting them, so that I came home to the chant of "C-h-a-r-l-e-s" or "e-n-o-u-g-h, enough!"

My first book, *Ah Fu, a Chinese River Boy*, was about life aboard a junk. Miss Herd promised that when I could read it all the way through to her, the book would be mine. It was a great incentive. Meanwhile my mother read stories to me about Noah's Ark, David and Goliath, and Jacob and the ladder up to heaven; and taught me to say my prayers, which went, "O Lord, please bless Mummy and Daddy and Susan and Jan, and all my friends and relations; I thank Thee for a lovely day, and please help me to be a good boy tomorrow."

I was not always a good boy tomorrow. I played mothers and fathers with some of my little friends, and when I got home my mother asked why my grey pullover was on back to front and inside out. At the height of the war shortages when, if you said "egg" to me I would think only of a square tin with a lid that was difficult to get off unless you had strong fingernails and a lot of determination, my friend Nonny Garner, who lived in the big house above the Hutch, discovered a bucket of fresh eggs obtained by his mother on the black market. Nonny, who had half an inch of yellow snot hanging permanently out of his left nostril, said you should always break an egg to see if it was bad or not, so we casually threw a dozen or so against the garage wall before getting bored and moving on to another game.

I was given a cast-off Indian suit and a tent for my birthday, and my mother helped me collect birds' feathers, which she sewed into a magnificent headdress. I refused to wear her first attempt, which was a single feather worn at the back of the head. This, I explained, was the headdress of an Indian squaw, not a chief, and simply would not do.

She helped me pitch the tent close to the water's edge and to build a fire, which she said had to be lit with only one match. (In her early years, she had been Brown Owl to one of the first Brownie groups, founded by Lady Baden-Powell).

When we moved to Beckside Cottage a few months later, I decided to have a go at lighting a fire all on my own; and there was just the place for it: a dry, dark tunnel under the laurel bushes that ran up from the garden gate to the side of the house. I collected plenty of dry twigs and made a wigwam of them as I had been taught. It lit with one match, as did the laurel bushes. The fire spread very rapidly. I beat a hasty retreat and ran back to the house to tell my Mummy, who formed a one-woman bucket chain and put it out.

My mother never lost her temper, never complained, and never meted out punishment. Nevertheless, although I desperately wanted to impress her, do well for her, and astonish her with my ability, I never seemed able to achieve this, and was ever conscious that I could never take my father's place in her affections. If I brought her something I had made or written or drawn, for which I wanted her praise, although she might congratulate me with a "Jolly fine!" I always felt that she was saying not what she really meant, but what she believed I wanted to hear. The hard truth was that there could be only one man in her life—my absent father. There is a photograph of him, bronzed from his time in West Africa, sitting on a boulder in the garden above the lake, with Jan leaning lovingly over his knee and little Charles (for it is I) lurking like a secret agent in the background.

Mother was a great letter writer. As well as writing every week to JG, she also wrote to Susan at Huyton College boarding school, her sister in Northern Rhodesia, her cousins in Glamorganshire, friends from her nursing days at University College Hospital, and her great friend Queenie White, whose husband Earnest was a Harley Street psychiatrist.

She eked out the rations, cooked for the three lodgers and us three children, and when we became owners of a black mongrel, it was Mother who housetrained her and delivered her litter of six puppies, four of which she drowned in a bucket. One thing she did not do while we were in the Lake District was to take us to church. We did go once, but the vicar stuttered so badly and went on for so long that my mother said "never again."

The occasions when she indulged herself in any sort of relaxation or entertainment (apart from her sketching of the distant hills) were few. But when I was five, she took me to see *Mrs. Miniver* at the cinema in Bowness-on-Windermere. It was the first time I had ever seen a film, but my mother inadvertently made it far more terrifying by covering my eyes during scenes that hinted of violence. However, I did see the evocative sequence in which the little ships make their way out of the Thames Estuary on their way to pick up the soldiers from the beaches of Dunkirk.

There was a price to pay for that trip to the cinema, as soon afterwards I began having recurring nightmares. One was of a German soldier lying half-concealed under our garden hedge. The other was much worse and I used to awake from it screaming. It was of a ghastly white eye that came closer and closer and closer until it was all I could see and—worse by far—it saw all of me.

The garden at The Hutch ran down to the water's edge, where there was a small jetty, from which I used to catch minnows in a jam jar. Next door was Borwick's boat yard, which was closed up for the duration of the war; but we children managed to squeeze under one of the boatshed doors and Susan set up her private study in the cabin of one of the motor cruisers, where she kept her writing case and her secret letters and essays. I found a pot of paintbrushes, but no paint, in the boatshed, so I made do with mud, which I mixed myself and applied thickly to the pristine, white hull.

One summer morning towards the end of the war, Susan came back to the house with horror writ clear on her brow. Mr. Borwick had opened the boat shed doors and the motor cruiser with her writing case (and, I believe, an incomplete novel) had gone. I was also disappointed, because I had not finished my work of repainting the boat. Mother used to say that if a job was worth doing, it was worth doing well. I agreed with her. It was very irritating. I like to finish things.

We took over ownership of two cats while we stayed at The Hutch. Judy was grey and Billy, who I adored, was black. When we moved to Beckside Cottage, Judy did a runner, but we took Billy with us and on arrival buttered his paws so that he would not run away. He was not, however, a good boy tomorrow. He took to staying out all night and he got into fights. You could hear him in the middle of the night, yowling and growling. One morning he came in for his breakfast after a night on the tiles looking much the worse for wear. His ear was bleeding, and there was a nasty wound on his chest. Mother tried to get hold of him, but he was too quick for her and disappeared rapidly over the stonewall at the back of the house.

There followed several weeks of sightings of Billy, and at each sighting his now suppurating chest injury looked worse. Eventually Mother decided that he must be put down, so she engaged the services of one of the few local men left in that part of England, and together they spent an afternoon playing hide and seek with Billy. This was not made easier by the appearance of another black cat with a white marking on its chest, which, on a fast-moving feline, looked exactly like Billy's septic wound. Our man eventually managed to capture Billy, but just as he was about to put him in the back of his van, Billy leapt to freedom and high tailed it back to the fells.

A week later, JG came home on forty-eight hour leave. He smelled of tobacco and boot polish and Imperial Leather soap, and when he went to the lavatory, it sounded (in the final stages of the operation) as if he were drilling holes in the floorboards. He didn't have much to do with me and I had little to do with him, though I did get to watch him strop his safety razor, lather his face, and, very scratchily, shave.

On the second morning of his visit, Billy Bones appeared sitting on the garden wall at the back of the house. My father took him a sardine on a plate. He also took his service revolver. He stroked Billy, talked gently to him, and, while Billy picked delicately at the sardine, shot him through the head.

My mother abhorred the practice of buying food on the black market as it prejudiced the war effort and took food from the mouths of those who needed it most. However, at Beckside cottage, we were fortunate to live next door to a farm, whose owner spoke with a Westmorland accent so broad that we couldn't understand him. We collected milk from him every day in a stainless steel can, which my mother always let stand for the cream to rise. She then poured it off, thick and yellow, and we had it on our porridge at breakfast.

Another supplement to our diet was wild fruit. Judy, our glossy black mongrel, was particularly useful as a sniffer-out of wild strawberries and raspberries, though she had no time at all for blackberries.

Mother, Jan, and I were picking blackberries one afternoon in a narrow lane where the brambles were loaded with fruit. We had filled two jars and were turning for home when we were accosted by a red-faced farmer who told my mother that she had no right to the blackberries, as they grew on his land. She pointed out that there were still many blackberries left and that many were still to ripen. But he was adamant and demanded that she handed them over at once.

"Very well," said my mother, "You may have your blackberries, but you will not have our labor." And with that, she threw the blackberries in the mud at his feet, grabbed my hand, turned on her heel, and left the farmer close to apoplexy.

4

Early in 1944, JG was posted to the training staff for the D-day landings, with responsibility for training sappers in the art of positioning Mulberry Harbors off the coast of Normandy, alongside which supply ships would unload munitions and stores for the Allied advance into France.

It was about this time that I first became aware that there was a war going on and that my father was part of it. I was given a picture book for children, which showed various scenes of heroism in the Navy, Army, and Air Force. One was of hundreds of soldiers wearing their tin hats, wading out up to their shoulders to the little boats that lay off the beaches of Dunkirk. Another was of sailors holding torches and revolvers as they boarded the German prison ship *Altmark* at night to break out the prisoners of war held on board. A third, which was my favorite, was of an RAF rear gunner fighting a fire in the back of a Lancaster bomber, one hand held up against his face against the heat of the flames.

Sometimes at night we heard heavy bombers flying low overhead. I believe these may have been the bombers of the RAF's Dam Buster squadron, practicing dummy runs for the raids on German reservoirs with Barnes-Wallis' bouncing bombs.

There was a big oak tree stump on high ground overlooking the boat sheds at the Hutch, and this I turned into my personal aircraft. When I saw a Spitfire fly at full throttle along the length of the lake, and then climb up and perform a magnificent victory roll, I was captivated.

In the spring of 1945, we moved from The Hutch to a remote log cabin on Tower Hill, which Susan, who took her role of elder sister very seriously, renamed Windy Top. The bungalow had no proper plumbing. There was an outside privy, and our water supply came from the peat-brown stream that tumbled downhill beside the bungalow. We bathed in a large metal saucer filled with water heated in kettles over a stove that ran on bottled gas.

Judy was in her element here. She used to dash off after rabbits and return hours later, panting twenty to the dozen, her tongue hanging out, and blood stains on her chops. One evening she did not come back. When we had called and whistled for some time, Mother led the way down the hill and into the woods on the other side of the main road, where we knew she hunted. In a silence between our calling and whistling, we heard a yelp. There was another long silence then another yelp. We headed towards these intermittent yelps and eventually found Judy hanging, unconscious, from her back paws from the top of a wire fence, which she must have tried to jump and failed to clear.

She recovered within a day or two and went back to her hunting, her yelps of excitement echoing to us through the trees.

JG landed in Normandy ten days after D-Day and on July 14, 1944 marched at the head of one of the first Bastille Day parades since the beginning of the war. After working on the staff of SHAFE (Supreme Headquarters Allied Forces Europe) for a few months, he was sent to Norway where he was engaged upon the re-establishment of local government in remote towns and villages among the fjords. He did a great deal of sailing, and when he eventually came home he brought with him a medal from the Oslo Sailing Club and two Elk knives, one for himself and the other, which he had blunted, for me. He also brought an ugly little black metal ashtray with the figure of a man carrying skis over his shoulder, which he used constantly until the end of his life.

I had been reared from my earliest years on stories not only of Noah and the Ark, David and Goliath, and Esau and Jacob, but of Mrs. Tiggywinkle, Squirrel Nutkin, and Peter Rabbit, which, like Arthur Ransome's first two books, were set in the Lake District. I recognized the Westmorland hills my mother sketched in the picture of Mrs. Tiggwinkle delivering the laundry, and, having often seen red squirrels, I could imagine them using their tails to sail before the wind across the lake to go and taunt Old Mr. Brown.

In the realm of literature, there seemed to be a grey area between truth and make-believe that led me to develop a healthy skepticism about the printed word. The problem was compounded by the fact that my mother was a great reader of novels, A.J. Cronin, R.F. Delderfield, Pearl S. Buck, and Richard Llewellyn being among her favorite authors. Some books she declared "good." I wanted to know *why* they were good—particularly the ones that brought a tear to her eye when she reached the last page and caused her to remark, sadly, "She dies."

I didn't really know what was real and what was not. Mother read Arthur Ransome's *Swallows and Amazons* and *Swallowdale* to me, and it puzzled me that, while Susan corresponded to Susan, Jan to Titty and Roger to myself, we didn't have an elder brother to take John's part. To make matters more complicated, Susan (my sister) had made up new names for the landmarks referred to in the

Arthur Ransome stories, so there was a continual conflict between the names in the book and the names we used. When I graduated to Arthur Ransome's *Missee Lee*, a further problem arose, because I could not get my head round the possibility that, while Swallows and Amazons referred to real places that I knew—albeit under other names—the names in *Missee Lee* did not refer to any real places or people. (The problem of names and their reference was clarified for me, many years later, when I read Frege's essay "On Sense and Reference" at Durham University.)

If I identified with any of the fictional characters that populated my formative years, it was probably Winnie-the-Pooh, because, with two elder sisters who seemed to know absolutely everything, I was painfully aware of my intellectual inadequacy. My aim in life was to be a good boy tomorrow and to be both an HB (helpful bear) and a BB (brave bear). Above all, I wanted to impress my Mummy.

A week or so before my seventh birthday we borrowed a rowing boat and went across Lake Windermere for a picnic. We tied the boat up, sat on a pebble beach, and ate scrambled egg sandwiches. Sitting on a branch that overhung the water, Jan said something about the war being over, and it was then that I learnt that an atomic bomb had been dropped on Japan. Moments after this revelation there was a flash of lightning and a clap of thunder. I was sitting next to my mother and burst into tears. I began stroking her arm, which had a burn scar on it from when she was a little girl. She rebuked me sternly for being afraid of a thunderstorm. But she did not understand: I was not crying because I was afraid for myself but because I was afraid that something might happen to her and I would be unable to protect her.

Was there more to it than that? Perhaps I sensed the horror of Hiroshima that hot, thundery afternoon when we picnicked by Lake Windermere, and it was then that the seeds of pacifism were planted.

It started to rain. We packed up the picnic and swimming things, got into the boat, and cast off. With my mother at the oars, we set out for the opposite shore, about a mile distant. The rain turned into a downpour and squalls swept down on us from the western hills, whipping the lake up into a fury. Mother made me lie down in the bottom of the boat and my sisters started baling. Susan led us in a rendering of a rousing hymn and, while the lightning cracked and the thunder banged back and forth across the lake, my mother heaved valiantly on the oars.

On the first Easter Sunday after the war ended, when the road was busy with traffic and Judy had gone off hunting, we heard a sudden scream of brakes. We rushed down the hill and found Judy lying at the side of the road. As we approached, she lifted her head for a moment, wagged her tail, and died.

We carried her up the hill, dug a shallow grave and buried her in the woods that she loved, with stones from the stream heaped in a little cairn to mark the spot. My mother and sisters cried for days afterwards, but although I tried very hard to follow suit I was unable to enter into the spirit of the thing. By that time I had the beginnings of an idea about the concept of life after death, and scandalized Jan by remarking that Judy was "up there" in heaven. "Dogs don't go to heaven," she said severely. "They don't have souls." I wanted to know how she knew they didn't have souls, but sensed that it was the sort of question one should not ask.

I walked, and later cycled, back and forth to school with Jan, who became my sole authority on questions of spiritual belief, morals, and ethics. She left me in no doubt that there were some matters—all of which seemed to be connected either with sex or money—that were not permitted subjects for discussion. When she heard me singing a popular song that went, "You made me love you, I didn't want to do it," she told me, a little darkly, that it was a bad song and I should not sing it. This intensified my curiosity. I wanted to know why it was a bad song and what it was the singer didn't want to do. But, once again, I saw that I was on dangerous ground and kept my questions to myself.

In September 1946, when I was eight years old, I learnt that we were to leave the Lake District and go to live in our house in London. The news came as a bolt from the blue. I had presumed that we would always live in the Lake District, because that was where we lived: I had no idea that we had a house in London.

We had a good clear out before departure, in the course of which Jan and I discovered a two-handled saw which we used to cut off the end of a birch log to take with us to London as a memento. We varnished it and it served as a doorstop at 67 Brent Way for sixty years.

On the day of our departure, when the taxi was due to arrive at any minute, I walked out alone through the trees to a clearing and looked for the last time over Lake Windermere to the Langdale Pikes, which my mother had so often sketched. I knew that our imminent departure marked a most important turning point in my life; that a chapter was over and a new chapter beginning—and I was overcome by a surge of what the Portuguese call *saudade*: an overwhelming feeling of sadness mixed with nostalgia, and the hopelessness of knowing that the past can never be recovered.

I heard my mother call.

"Charles!"

It was at that moment, on hearing my name called, that I recognized myself, as John Locke puts it in *An Essay Concerning Human Understanding* as "a thinking intelligent being that has reason and reflection and can consider itself as itself, the same thinking thing in different times and places."

I had become a person.

5

67 Brent Way was (and still is) a three-up, three-down terraced house half a mile down the hill from West Finchley tube station—foursquare, as Peter Sellers would have it, on the Northern Line. It boasted a small front garden behind a privet hedge and a narrow back garden. The back lane was separated by iron railings from the allotments, whose owners grew everything from turnips to tobacco. A broad stream, the River Dollis, ran along below the allotments, and beyond its steep clay banks was the Finchley Golf Course.

Much had changed in our eight-year absence. A doodlebug (V-1 rocket) had fallen on the hard courts of the Finchley Lawn Tennis Club, a hundred yards from our house. Garden fences had been blown down, roofs laid open to the sky, and the tennis pavilion demolished. Our back lawn had been converted to a vegetable patch, where a few bedraggled rows of spinach, potatoes, and leeks struggled up through weeds. Worst of all, we had squatters: the Harvey's, who occupied the ground floor and were refusing to move out.

Although I was eight years old at the time, I have no recollection of the journey south from Windermere or our arrival at Number Sixty-seven. I must have blocked it out. My first memory is of playing my father's old gramophone records in the upstairs front bedroom with Jan. He had a curious collection. There was one that made fun of "the Portuguese, the Armenians, and the Greeks" and another, sung by a Chinese woman with a squeaky voice, whose words sounded like:

> Oh sing-a-loo
> And a how do you do
> At the morning time of hour!
> We don't know who we are,
> We don't know who we are—
> Oh sing-a-loo
> And a how do you do
> At the morning time of hour!

Another, which was chipped, had a duet in close harmony from Gilbert and Sullivan's operetta *Iolanthe*. There was also one I considered very boring. It was by a German. Beethoven. I didn't like the Germans. It was thanks to them that we were huddled up in three small rooms with bare floorboards.

The bathroom, which we shared with the Harvey's, sported the only hot water tap in the house. Water was heated in a furred up electric geyser. On turning on the tap, steam would issue forth in clouds for some time before bursting forth, close to boiling point, in a thin, superheated dribble.

The Harvey's claimed that we were "bomb dodgers" and as such had no right to repossess our house. As far as I was concerned, the only redeeming feature of this arrangement was that my mother was obliged to share her bed with me, as the smallest bedroom had been turned into a kitchen.

After a couple of months my mother donned her best (and only) tweed suit, put on her best (and only) pearl necklace and her best (and only) pair of court shoes, and went to Barnet for what she called "the case" to have the Harvey's evicted—which, after quite a lot of legal wrangling, they were, so that for the first time since our arrival back in London we were able to enter our dining room, sitting room, kitchen, and back garden.

JG came home from the war in April 1947 and the sound of holes being drilled in the floorboards emanated once more from what we called the "lav." Jan and Susan moved to the back bedroom, I was ousted from my mother's bed, and the bronzed interloper back from India, who kept his shaving brush in a chipped enamel mug, who smoked Players cigarettes, and whose military bearing, authority, and pungent body odor pervaded the house, moved in.

I did not decide to become "difficult." It just happened. Nor was I aware of being difficult, only that from the moment of my father's arrival at 67 Brent Way, the sunshine went out of my life. Having experienced peace during the idyllic war years by Lake Windermere, I now found myself conscripted into a strange sort of war in time of peace.

Within minutes of his arrival, this stranger I called "Daddy" gave me a second hand Meccano set, to which I took an immediate dislike. But I wanted to please him, and struggled desperately to be interested and delighted with the horrible collection of assorted metalwork.

He bent over me, the wind whistling through the black wires that grew out of his nose, and showed me how to use the little spanner to tighten the nuts onto the bolts, and how to put a washer in between so that they wouldn't work loose. He gave me a well-thumbed manual with instructions and plans for making an antiquated looking car, an airplane that would never fly, and a crane that toppled over when you tried to lift anything heavier than a cotton reel with it. Then, with a few clipped words of man-to-man encouragement, Daddy left me and went upstairs to be with my mother. I went down on my knees on the bare boards of the front room and shed hot tears. After a while, my mother came down to see what the matter was. She was unable to conceal her annoyance, and when my father came to the door and our eyes met, I knew that he was my rival.

Everything changed after that. Nothing was ever the same again.

For a few months the house remained almost bare of furniture, and my only link with the past was the log that Jan and I had sawn off on our last day in the Lake District, which was now used to keep the dining room door open while my mother rushed in and out, waiting on us like a skivvy.

One day our furniture arrived from the store, and with it my father's books, which were lodged in glass-fronted bookcases in the front room on either side of the gas fire. He was an avid and eclectic reader. In the bookcase to the left of the gas fire, he had Gibbon's *Decline and Fall,* Kant's *Critique of Pure Reason,* and a complete set of Ruskin's essays on art. He had most of the plays of Bernard Shaw, including one volume entitled *Plays Unpleasant,* a title I found intriguing. His ink-stained copy of *Treasure Island* was there, along with *Midshipman Easy* and *An Awfully Big Adventure.* There were French, German and Urdu dictionaries, volumes of poetry by Yeats, Wordsworth, Coleridge, and Browning—but, oddly enough, no Shakespeare. There were two volumes on how to make a scale model of the Cutty Sark, a book about mountaineering, one about a dwarf, which my mother had been forbidden to read while pregnant with Jan, and a handsome first edition of *All About Ships* by Lieut. Tapprell Dorling, R.N., which had been presented to James G. Wheeler in December 1913 at Bexhill School as junior prize for religious knowledge.

In the bookcase to the right of the gas fire, my father kept heavy tomes about prophecy, eschatology, and New Testament theology by eminent Plymouth Brethren like John Nelson Darby, Blair Neatby, and Charles Müller. He was able to take a book down from a shelf and turn immediately to the reference or quotation he needed. On the rare occasions that I was allowed to touch these books, I was taught to be very careful how to turn the pages: never from the bottom corner, always from the top of the far edge. A book was never to be placed open and face down, nor was anything thicker than a slip of paper to be used as a marker. The printed word was holy.

The arrival of furniture and books had a curious effect on the family. Until that time, my mother had been the center of our lives. Now, she abdicated that position in favor of my father, whose authority and apparent infallibility, with the arrival of his modest library, were immeasurably increased. So it was that, within a matter of weeks of my father's return, the atmosphere in our family changed from being relaxed, creative, and outgoing, to being perfectionist, dogmatic, and introverted.

It was about this time that I learnt that we were PBs. Later, I learnt that our sect—though we never referred to it as such—was divided into two sub-sects, the Exclusive Brethren, and the Open Brethren, and that we were members of the latter. Exclusive Brethren, I learnt, had nothing to do with the outside world, and excluded any member of the sect who did, while Open Brethren were more relaxed.

But only a little. As a family, we separated ourselves from the world in several important ways. We looked down with hubristic disdain on the Church of England and all Christian sects that did not practice baptism by immersion; we regarded ourselves as better read and more intelligent, witty, artistic, and creative than most people; and, although we were desperately hard up, we regarded wealth as a mark of worldliness, and looked askance at those whom we termed "comfortably off." To top it all, it was obvious to anyone who met him that my father was an officer and a gentleman—a lieutenant colonel, no less—whose rank appeared before his name in the cellophane window of the bills, reminders, and final warnings that fell onto our front door mat with monotonous regularity.

In addition to a sideboard and dining room table, two more items of furniture were crammed into our cluttered front room. There was a Selfridges upright piano upon which, very occasionally, my mother played hymns, one of which she used to sing to me that went:

> Jesus bids us shine with a clear pure light,
> Like a little candle, burning in the night.

The other item of furniture was an oak bureau, whose roll-top rolled off soon after its arrival, and was never replaced, so that it was permanently open with the clutter of my father's papers, tools, and oddments permanently on view.

The front room was not only a dining room but an office, library, music room, and workshop. Later, it became a printer's shop, with a cabinet of little boxes of lead print, tubes of ink, a marble block, and quantities of assorted cards and paper.

That room was also our window on the world. It was like a bird watcher's hide, only we watched people rather than birds, and we didn't bother to hide. Its modest bay window looked outward and upward on the passers-by. Just as we had given names to the landmarks in the Lake District, so we now gave names to our fellow residents in Brent Way. Our arrogance and self-satisfaction knew no bounds. There was Charlie Come-Come, Soppy Date, Heffy, and Trip the Fool. Passers-by who were foolish enough to glance in at us would look quickly away, nervous of our hilarity.

Thus was planted in me a feeling that we were in every way superior to and separate from the rest of humanity. I even wondered if the head of King George VI on a penny piece had been sculpted in my father's likeness, though King George did not have a mustache, and looked younger than my father.

But—what a ridiculous comparison! We were far superior to the royal family because we, being Open Brethren, were entirely confident that we would be caught up at the Rapture to be forever with the Lord, while the royal family, being only Church of England, had no such guarantee.

6

Soon after my father's return from the war we joined the assembly of saints at Oakleigh Hall in Whetstone, and my Sundays became filled with journeys to and from the morning meeting for the breaking of bread, the afternoon Crusaders' Sunday school class in Woodside Park, and the Gospel service in the evening, also at Oakleigh Hall. This sudden lurch into religiosity came as an unpleasant shock: for the first time I was led to believe that I was stained with original sin, and that if I did not accepted Christ as my savior, I would go to hell for all eternity.

Sundays were full of tension, and I came to detest them. The day started in a flurry of activity as we prepared ourselves for the morning meeting. Susan and Jan had to do their ablutions and decide what to wear and my father had to strop his razor, wash, shave, and polish his and my mother's shoes—all before breakfast. Breakfast over, something little short of panic set in as the 10:15 departure time approached. Susan hates her hat. My father can't find his leather gloves. Jan is taking an age in the bathroom, while I lurk about, keeping my head low to avoid the crossfire. And so we set out, Susan and Jan walking ahead, my mother arm-in-arm with my father, and holding my hand. By unspoken agreement, my father and I walk in step with my mother, he shortening his step, I lengthening mine. Each member of the family carries a Bible. Mine has been awarded to me for one hundred consecutive attendances at Crusaders' Sunday school.

We walk up Fursby Avenue to West Finchley tube station, buy our tickets, wait for the tube to trundle in from Finchley Central, and travel two stops up to Totteridge, from where we walk about a mile to Oakleigh Hall. We arrive at five to eleven and take our seats, which are arranged round the Lord's Table, laid with a decanter of wine, two silver goblets, a cottage loaf, and two silver platters. I sit next to my mother; next to her is my father, then Jan, then Susan. Our seats, which are at the head of the hall by the pulpit, face the main body of the congregation, so that we are in the view of most of the assembly.

Women wear hats, but no make up or jewelry. The meeting starts at eleven o'clock in silence. My father leans forward in his seat and buries his head in his hands. He keeps his fingernails long, and his forefingers are stained with nicotine.

He has a mustache, clipped like a toothbrush, and bushy eyebrows that grow out in spikes.

We wait—sometimes for five minutes or more—for the Holy Spirit to lead us. Eventually one of the brethren invites us to turn to a chapter and verse in Holy Scripture—perhaps an obscure passage about sacrificial procedure from the Book of Leviticus. Readings before the breaking of bread tend to be from the Old Testament; readings after, from the New. Or, perhaps one of the brethren is prompted by the Holy Spirit to lead us in prayer. When old Mr. Henry prays in his wheezy voice, I count how many times he says "in this scene here below."

From the first scripture reading a theme is developed. The whole service is supposed to be guided by the Holy Spirit, but preparation takes place all the same. More readings, prayers, and hymns follow. When a hymn is announced, we get to our feet and my father starts us off, supported enthusiastically by Susan, Jan, and my mother. There is no accompaniment.

Most of this goes straight over my head, and what doesn't is so boring that my mind descends into a sort of numbness. Time passes with interminable slowness. At last, as midday approaches, one of the elder brethren—sometimes my father, but usually Mr. Finch—rises from his seat and approaches the table. He prays aloud for some while, then reverently takes the cottage loaf and breaks it in four, placing two pieces on each of the silver platters. These are passed round, and all those in communion (which is to say they have been publicly baptized by immersion) pinch a small piece of bread out of the loaf and eat it, immediately bowing their heads in prayer. Neither Susan, Jan, nor I have been baptized, so we do not take communion. After a minute or two, Mr. Finch approaches the table again, murmurs another prayer, and pours the wine into the two goblets, which are also passed round.

But the Sunday morning meeting is not yet over. After the breaking of bread, a collection is taken. The Brethren teaching is that we should give one tenth of our income to the Lord. My father puts a ten-shilling note into the scarlet bag. I have been provided with a sixpenny piece to put in it.

There's a long pause after the collection bags have been put on the Communion table, propped against the salver with the remains of the bread. It comes to an end when one of the elder brethren gets to his feet and expounds the scriptures for at least ten minutes, and often more.

With luck—or, as the Brethren would say, God willing—we are out by twenty past twelve, and after making our good mornings to Mr. Minto (we call him Sucky Minto behind his back), Tom Harrison, Mr. Henry, Queenie Finch, Mr. and Mrs. Warner, and Anne Wright, we set out on the trek back to Totteridge station, where we have just missed the train and have to wait on the platform ten minutes for the next one. Out we get at West Finchley, and down Fursby Avenue we march, Bibles in hand, to return to Number Sixty-seven, where we lunch on cold meat and mashed potatoes. Over lunch, my parents discuss the content of the meeting, which usually includes an assessment as to whether various speakers were, or were not, "good." Such discussions might start with my mother remarking something like, "I thought Tom Harrison was quite good on sanctification, didn't you, Jim?"

Each of the three siblings has a special relationship with each other and with our parents. Jan is my father's darling; I am his rival; Susan is his problem. I am my mother's darling; Jan is her rival; Susan is her problem. Susan is passionate, quick-tempered, witty, and academic. Jan is phlegmatic, dreamy, and artistic. I am secretive, deceitful, self-seeking, and sex-obsessed.

After Sunday lunch, my mother makes tea and we assemble in the small sitting room by the fire to listen to Ludwig Koch's recordings of songbirds on the wireless, while my father flips through the pages of *Echoes of Service*, a missionary magazine. At two thirty, I have to start getting ready for Crusaders. I leave at twenty to three, and go by bike to Woodside Park.

It's a boys' Sunday school. I wear the Crusader's shield-shaped badge in the lapel of my grey jacket. We are split into two teams, Jets and Rockets (I am a Jet) and compete to find texts in the Bible, points being awarded as air miles traveled to the moon, an idea that I regard as absurd. We sing choruses of our own choice, a favorite being:

> He lives! He lives!
> Christ Jesus lives today!
> He walks with me, he talks with me,
> Along life's narrow way;
> He lives! He lives!
> Salvation to impart;
> You ask me how I know he lives—
> He lives within my heart!

When we've sat through a short sermon from the Crusader leader and have sung a few more choruses, it's over, and I'm riding hell-for-leather back home, where my mother has made butterfly cakes with home-made blackberry jam for tea.

After tea there's a brief respite before it's time to set out for the evening meeting, otherwise known as The Gospel. The evening meeting is intended principally for unbelievers, though these are few and far between. It starts at six o'clock with gospel hymns selected from *Golden Bells* or *Sankey's Sacred Songs and Solos*, and we are accompanied on the organ by Queenie Finch. Susan likes to show off her musical ability by singing the descant, and Mrs. Warner, who has a yellow complexion and an enlarged thyroid gland, swoops up to her notes. Queenie Finch pumps away at the organ foot pedals and we sing:

> There is a green hill far away
> Beyond the city wall,
> Where our dear Lord was crucified,
> And died to save us all.
>
> We may not know, we cannot tell
> What pain he had to bear;
> But we believe 'twas for our sakes
> He hung and suffered there.

After half an hour of gospel hymns, a sermon is preached, sometimes by a visiting speaker but more usually by one of the Oakleigh Hall brethren. The message is always a variation on the same theme. Reconciliation between God and Man after Adam's disobedience in the Garden of Eden (in 4004 BC) is only possible through the shedding of the blood of Jesus on the Cross, and those who, having heard the gospel, do not accept Him as their Savior, are destined to spend an eternity in hell, as forecast in the Book of Revelation.

The Gospel draws to a close. After one last hymn and a final prayer, we set off home again via another trip in the tube from Totteridge to West Finchley and another walk down Fursby Avenue to 67 Brent Way. Supper is scrambled eggs on toast, upon which my father sprinkles a little curry powder to remind him, I daresay, of happier times in India. After supper my sisters are allowed stay up and listen to the wireless.

"Bed," says my mother, looking my way. "School tomorrow."

"O Lord," I pray, "I thank thee for a lovely day. Bless Mummy and Daddy and Susan and Jan and all my friends and relations. Help me to work hard at school and be a good boy tomorrow, and if it be thy will, let me get into UCS, for I ask this in the name of the Lord Jesus. Amen."

My father occasionally preached the Gospel at other assembly halls and sometimes in the street when gospel missions were under way. I once suffered the agony of standing out in the road with him while he preached to passers by who scurried past looking the other way.

He was meticulous in his preparation of his Gospel sermons. One set of notes, which I found among his papers, is made on War Office stationery under the wildly inappropriate printed heading, *Any further communication on this subject should be addressed to The Under Secretary of State, The War Office*:

1. Man is naturally SINFUL—Romans 8, v. 1-7

2. and is therefore spiritually DEAD—Ephesians 2, v. 1

3. Being CONVICTED of sin, however—Luke 15 v. 18

4. he REPENTS—Matthew 21 v. 28-29

5. and CONFESSES his sin to Christ—1 John, 1, v.9

6. He is then REDEEMED—1 Peter 1, v. 18-19

7. by the PROPITIATORY SACRIFICE OF JESUS CHRIST—Galatians 3, v.13

8. through FAITH—Ephesians 2 v. 8

9. in his BLOOD—Romans 3 v. 23-25

10. and is FORGIVEN—1 John 1 v. 9

11. and JUSTIFIED in the sight of God—Romans 4, and 5, v. 1

12. He becomes REGENERATE (a new creature)—2 Corinthians 5, v. 17

13. Having ACCEPTED eternal life by faith as a gift—Romans 6, v.23

14. and is SANCTIFIED (made holy)—2 Corinthians 5, v.20

15. by the HOLY SPIRIT—1 Corinthians 3, v.16

16. who DELIVERS from sin—Romans 6, v. 14

17. gives VICTORY over temptation—1 Corinthians 10, v. 13

18. helps him to SERVE God—John 15, v.8

19. and GLORIFY God—John 15, v.8

20. He WATCHES for Christ's return—Mark 13 v. 34-37

21. in order, finally, TO BE WITH HIM—Philemon 1 v. 23

Another page is devoted to dispelling doubts that Christians might have about their faith. Under the heading, *I'm told the Bible can't be trusted* he notes:

1. Science is weak through lack of conclusive evidence.

2. Science revises; the Bible remains—e.g. Flood.

3. Archeology proves the Bible history true.

4. Fulfilled prophecy proves it is God-inspired.

5. Its Gospel has a unique power to change men. This too is of God.

My discovery, years later, of these breathtakingly naïve notes was instrumental in opening my eyes to the absurdity of Christian belief. Christians tread a dangerous path when they appeal to science. They do better openly to admit that their religion is irrational and possible only by making a leap of faith "on the strength of the absurd" as Kierkegaard suggests in *Fear and Trembling*.

7

It must have been difficult for my father to make the transition from living in an officers' mess to sharing a small bomb-damaged house in the London suburbs with his wife and three children. I think he was very depressed after his return to Number Sixty-seven. He had been away for nearly eight years and his periods of home leave had been few and short. He brought all his military kit home with him, including his service revolver and two pouches of ammunition, one of which contained dum-dum bullets, banned by the Hague Convention. These he hid behind his stiff white collars in the drawer of his wardrobe—but of course, I found them. He smoked heavily, was moody, and suffered from frequent nightmares. One night at two o'clock in the morning, while fast asleep, he leapt out of bed, threw the window wide open, and shouted at the top of his voice down the road.

He abhorred round shoulders, whistling, suede shoes, Americans, telephones, Charles Dickens, television, Field Marshall Montgomery, women in trousers, Clement Attlee, and the Labor Party. He admired Ruskin, polished leather, good seamanship, J.S. Bach, woodwork, General Alexander, Churchill, and the Tories. He read the *Daily Telegraph* and the *Spectator* and smoked Players cigarettes. He banked at Lloyds Pall Mall (Guards and Cavalry) and wore the regimental tie of the Royal Engineers with his demobilization suit.

Weekdays started at 6:50 a.m. when my mother went down to make his morning cup of tea. Ten minutes later, I would hear him stropping his razor, and he would occupy the bathroom for a further ten minutes while he shaved. He would then bark, 'Bathroom's free!' whereupon Susan (who was nearly always in a hurry) would dash in and lock the door behind her. Out she would come some time later, and would bring my father's wrath down upon her head if she did not similarly chirrup, 'Bathroom's free!' Then it was Jan's turn, and then it was mine. Into my woolen vest and woolen underpants, on with my second-hand short grey trousers, second-hand grey shirt, and school tie; and on with my second-hand school blazer and second-hand shoes and long grey socks kept up with garters that left a red mark under my knee at the end of the day.

Ours was a family divided by questions of Lilliputian dimensions. Should milk be poured on porridge before or after the sugar? Should milk go into tea, or tea into milk? Should boiled eggs be opened by bashing them on the top and peeling the shell off by hand, or by using a teaspoon to take the top off in one swipe? Such questions were the subject of earnest and sometimes heated debate. Over the years I came to the conclusion that my mother's ways of doing things were almost invariably superior to those of my father, whose conservatism and incessant striving for perfection often led him to do things in a more laborious and time consuming way than was necessary. He never learnt that excellence can, on occasion, be the enemy of the good.

The sitting room was at the back of the house and looked out over the allotments to the stream, with the Finchley golf course beyond. We had an ancient and rather uncomfortable sofa, for which my mother painstakingly made a fitted cover out of white canvas with terra cotta piping, and a beaten brass tray from India that was put up on legs when we had home baked flapjacks for tea. On the wall by the small open fire was a button you could press to ring for the maid, though the bell didn't work. Even if it had, no maid would have answered, as we didn't have one.

Our wireless was rented by the month, and it was our link to an outside world, with which we had a curiously ambivalent relationship. We listened to *Music While You Work*, *Have a Go* with Wilfred Pickles, *Workers Playtime*, *Family Favorites*, Tommy Handley in *Itma*, Richard Murdoch and Kenneth Horne in *Much Binding in the Marsh*, *Mrs. Dale's Diary*, *Dick Barton*, *In Town Tonight* and *Radio Newsreel*. And then there were *The Critics*, with Lionel Hale, who I met many years later when he was married to Crystal, daughter of the novelist A.P. Herbert, and they were living in Islington by the Regent's canal. Lionel very kindly read and commented on some of my early articles in *Blackwood's Magazine*. He entertained me in his upstairs sitting room to a glass of gin and lime, and boasted that he could write a short story in the style of his friend Somerset Maugham.

Soon after our arrival at 67 Brent Way, Susan started at Queen Elizabeth's Grammar School in High Barnet, while Jan and I went to Byron House, an arty, progressive school attended by children whose parents tended to be what my father termed "suede shoesy."

Jan and I set out for school each morning at a quarter past eight and walked up to West Finchley station where we took the tube to Highgate. The school stood in a leafy suburb a little way from Highgate village. Mr. and Mrs. Allen were headmaster and headmistress. My teacher was Miss Winkup, a smartly dressed lady who was generous with the lipstick and always immaculately turned out. Though she was an excellent teacher, I never related to her closely in the way I had with Miss Herd at Blackwell House. Her make-up seemed to act like a mask that separated me from the real person.

It was a happy school. The day started when we marched in to the same tune played by Mrs. Allen on the piano. It is a piece that I can sing to this day, but which I have never been able to name. We sit down cross-legged in rows on the floor, cozily close to one another, and Mrs. Allen or Miss Winkup reads a poem by Christina Rosetti about lambs jumping off their feet. We sing a secular song and then go to our classes to draw pictures, sing *Frère Jacques* or recite our times tables.

My best friends, Martin, Johnny, and Sammy, were respectively Anglo-Saxon, Jewish, and Syrian. I also discovered a passion for three little girls, Judith, Marion, and Sally. Judith was sexy, Marion was sisterly, but Sally was the one I wanted to marry. She had shiny dark pigtails tied with pink bows, a round, rosy-cheeked face, and a wonderful jollity about her that I found irresistible. I always tried to stand next to her in the milk queue at the mid-morning break. One day I was so overcome with love that I felt the need to demonstrate it in a positive way, so I gave her what I thought was a gentle uppercut to the chin. She burst into tears and avoided me from then on, and at the end of term there was a comment in my school report to the effect that I should in future seek to champion the weaker members of the community.

In the afternoons after lunch, we had to lie down on our blankets on the parquet floor of the main hall under the supervisory eye of Miss Winkup. Martin, Judith, and I shared blankets and put one over us so that we could explore each other in privacy.

My sexual experience was further extended, if that is the appropriate word, by the presence of a climbing rope that hung from a branch of a hornbeam tree in the school gardens. One lunch break while climbing the rope I experienced my first orgasm, a feeling so amazing that all I could do was to hang motionless, my legs tightly wrapped round the rope until it stopped and my pulse subsided. I became a keen and adept rope-climber after that.

8

I was small for my age and thin from the years of wartime austerity. One summer after a prolonged bout of influenza, I was sent to be fattened up with a distant relation, Muriel Poynder, who lived in a large house set in its own grounds at Woodham Ferrers in Essex. Auntie Mew was a large, tall lady who was generous to a fault. She was married to Sydney, who was as wizened and scraggy as she was buxom. He liked to ask me questions that I could never answer so that he could answer them for me. Auntie Mew's sister was Auntie Winifred, who had a respiratory complaint that made her voice sound like a penny whistle. She was known, appropriately enough, as Auntie Winnie.

The house and grounds were grand. There were sweeping lawns that ran down to a large goldfish pond with a punt, a walled garden, a peach orchard, and a small field where a solitary cow chewed the cud. Auntie Mew baked her own bread and churned her own butter; and Uncle Sydney pottered about turning lamp standards and bowls on a lathe in his workshop, or gave instructions to the handyman who was known as Caesar because of his habit of saying, "See, sir?"

During my stay I was joined by a distant cousin called Marianne, a dark haired, sensual girl two years my senior. One morning she got into bed with me and pressed herself against my back. She tried to persuade me to turn to face her so that we could have a hug. I had no experience of being hugged, and presumed that it was something rather sinful so, to my eternal regret, I turned away and, sanctimonious little prig that I was, ostentatiously opened my Bible and turned to the daily portion in the Old Testament that was appointed to be read in my Scripture Notes. Marianne did not try to conceal her disgust, and I have always regretted losing out on the cuddle that could have been ours. The trouble was that I had received so little tactile affection in my short life that I did not know how to give or receive it. If only I could have thrown my Bible and Scripture Notes on the floor, turned to Marianne, and let her take me in her arms.

I was fed clotted cream with my porridge for breakfast, home-churned butter with just about everything, and cakes made with double-yoked eggs. The consequence of so rich a diet was that soon after returning home I began complaining to my mother that I felt sick in the mornings. This made her laugh, though I didn't understand why. When my complaints continued, I was taken along to see the doctor, who looked at the whites of my eyes, took a sample of my urine and prodded my stomach. I was diagnosed as having a palpable liver and admitted to University College Hospital for observation—in the bad old days of 1949, there were plenty of hospital beds to go round, even for malingerers like me.

I was put into a men's medical ward. Mother brought me a Biggles book by W.E. Johns, and needles and wool to knit vests for African children on my aunt's mission station in Northern Rhodesia.

I fell in love with Nurse Pooley, a redhead with milk-white skin, who seemed more beautiful to me than it was possible for any human being to be. I listened to pop music on the hospital headphones: the lyrics "Flash, bang, alakazan, wonderful you came by" and "I'd like to get you on a slow boat to China" expressed my feelings towards Nurse Pooley exactly.

I enjoyed my time in hospital. I raced up and down the ward in a wheel chair, learnt what having your bowels open meant, heard cockney humor for the first time, and struck up a strange, silent acquaintance with an old man down at the end of the ward, who was very ill. He used to look at me with a sad, wistful smile. He held a sort of fascination for me, because he was so old and frail—and yet for all that there was still a twinkle of cheerfulness in his watery eyes. One morning I went down to the end of the ward to say hello to him, but his bed was stripped and empty, and Nurse Pooley would not tell me where he had gone.

9

In 1949, soon after my eleventh birthday, I started at Holly Hill, the junior branch of University College School, in the wealthy suburb of Hampstead. I was in a class of fifteen and a member of Simmonds House. We were taken for Music by Mr. Strong, Art by Mr. Smaggersgale, English by Mr. Dean, History by Mr. Byrom, and Arithmetic by Mr. Trendle. Merit points were awarded for good work, and at the House Meeting at the end of each week, our score of merit points was read out. I seldom won merit points for anything apart from English composition and rhyming verse. One of my efforts, which won two merit points, was called, at my mother's suggestion, *Nostalgia*:

> When I was very little
> And lived away from towns
> I used to do all sorts of things
> Among the lakes and downs.
> I learnt to swim; I learnt to skate;
> I also learnt to fish:
> And at the end of every day,
> I ate a tidy dish.
> But now I have to go to school
> And learn things every day;
> That's why I wish with all my heart
> That I could get away
> From London's busy traffic,
> From buses and from trains,
> Back to the lakes and downs and fells,
> And the little country lanes.

This piece was not entirely honest. What I really longed to get away from was the straightjacket of Christian discipline in which I now found myself.

I took the Eleven-Plus examination in English, Arithmetic, and General Knowledge soon after my arrival at UCS, but in spite of much coaching on Susan's part, failed in Arithmetic. This would have been unimportant had my parents had any money, but since coming back from the war, my father had been in and out of work and we lived hand to mouth from month to month. At one stage, things became so desperate that my father took a job as a commissionaire, and stood outside the Curzon Hotel in a long coat and top hat, opening taxi doors to the rich and famous, some of whom he recognized from his days in the Dragoon Guards.

My failure to pass the Eleven Plus exam was little short of a catastrophe, as it meant that I was faced with the horrific probability of being sent to a secondary modern school instead of staying on at UCS. I took the exam a second time and failed it again, whereupon my father decided to pull strings.

In the summer of 1950, I was required to attend an interview with an educational psychologist. I was taken to this interview by the headmaster, Mr. Vogel, who drew me aside before I went in and said, "The lady who will talk to you is very shy, Charles, so I want you to do your best to put her at her ease."

In I went, and was greeted by a woman completely at her ease who, in a conversational sort of way, led me into solving mental arithmetic problems rather in the same way that, in Plato's dialogue *Meno*, Socrates leads a servant into proving that the square on the hypotenuse is equal to the sum of the squares on the other two sides. I was required to read aloud to her (something I was good at) and when she asked me what I thought "piscatorial" meant, I had enough Latin to answer, "Something to do with fishes?"

Finally I had to tell her a story and draw a picture at the same time, so I concocted an entirely autobiographical tale about a nasty little boy who went for a walk with his dog and stole apples on the way, while drawing my favorite picture, which was of a sailing boat on Lake Windermere, with the hills rising up in the distance and smoke rising from the chimney of a little house with lattice windows, set in the heart of the forest.

I passed this test, and from then on, my school fees were paid by the State. But although the specter of a secondary modern education vanished and my father's financial problems were eased by my success, there lurked (and still lurks) within me a feeling of guilt at being made into a special case and getting in by the back door. There is, however, a coda to this little piece that rather puts the tin lid on the efficacy of educational tests, as I later became a member of Mensa with an IQ score of 152.

The family finances went from bad to worse, largely because my father was so scrupulously honest that he preferred to leave a job rather than compromise his principles. After trying his hand at selling cars, he joined a firm that specialized in sanding and polishing wooden floors; and when that job came to an end and he found himself unemployed again, he decided to take up printing.

He bought a hand printing press, along with a variety of lead typefaces, blocks, inks, and paper, and set about printing letterheads, invitations, menus, and invoices.

But, once again, his perfectionism held him back. Each printing block had to be set up by hand, packed out with blocks of wood called "furniture," and leveled on a marble block. He would then run off a proof, correct every error, re-fit the furniture, re-level the block, re-fit it in the machine, and try again. And, if necessary, again—*and again*!

One of his commissions was the letterhead for the Pelham Grill in South Kensington, which the customer wanted embossed. My father did not have an embossing capability but there was a cheap alternative method on the market, albeit a labor-intensive one. The effect was achieved by shaking what looked like gold dust on the wet ink and holding it up to the gas fire. Five thousand letterheads were required, and I was co-opted to assist in the operation of toasting each individual sheet just the right amount so that the gold dust bubbled up to produce the embossed effect.

In spite of his time in the Royal Engineers, he was more of a thinker than a mechanic, and was burdened with the belief that if a thing was worth doing, it had to be done not merely well, but perfectly. This lifelong dedication to the achievement of excellence was a ball and chain he dragged behind him. He was beset by hesitancy and lack of confidence. Everything he did, he did after deliberation. Even when he signed his name, the pen nib would hover uncertainly before making contact with the paper.

It would be easy, but quite misleading, to caricature him as an overbearing religious bigot. But he was not. He was an extraordinary mixture of worldliness and spirituality, the artistic and the mechanical, pride and self-denial, courage and humility. His intellect was at war with his religious faith, and his self-image as an officer and a gentleman was at war with his straightened circumstances. Only a few years before he had been a lieutenant colonel in India, playing polo, dining in the mess, and giving orders—and now he was breaking his long nails and getting his sensitive fingers covered in ink for the sake of achieving perfection in the production of two hundred immaculately printed invoices for a local building contractor.

The printing scheme was not a success. Things went from bad to worse. I was an inveterate poker and prier into my father's papers, and was shocked one day to discover a carbon copy of a letter he had sent to my headmaster explaining that he had had a setback in business, and asking to be given more time to pay outstanding fees, which amounted to over a hundred pounds. I was old enough to know very well that his "setback in business" was a monumental understatement. The fact of the matter was, we were on the rocks.

That letter planted in me a grim determination to make money, or at least stay solvent, that has stayed with me throughout my life. I persuaded my mother to let me start cycling to school to save the tube fares. I wanted to do a paper round, but my parents would not allow it as they considered it to be lower class and demeaning. But they did allow me to collect newspaper from friends and neighbors and sell it in bulk at a place in North Finchley; and I earned a weekly sixpence by supplying a sack of split fence wood to the Reverend G.T. Manley, a retired theologian and author of religious tomes.

At about the same time that I was taking and failing the eleven plus exam, I was voice tested for training as a choirboy for St Paul's cathedral, and offered a scholarship to St. Paul's School. I was very excited about this and keen to take it up, but my father turned it down because he did not want his son to be tainted by Anglicanism.

We slid, inexorably, down the slippery slope towards bankruptcy. Gas and electricity bills were never paid until the final reminder arrived. My father was unable to compete with established printing firms, and scarcely able to keep up the mortgage payments of six pounds a month on the house. To help make ends meet my mother started night nursing at Barnet hospital. She used to set out on her bicycle at seven in the evening, and I sometimes cycled out to meet her in the early morning, and we would ride back together to Number Sixty-seven.

One morning when we were on the very brink of bankruptcy, a letter arrived addressed to my mother from the Midland Bank. She read it, went pale, and handed it up the table to my father, who sat in the revolving chair with his back to the bureau with the broken roll-top front. The letter informed my mother that a donor who wished to remain anonymous had decided to send her ten pounds per month until further notice.

This was considered to be an answer to prayer, as was the load of logs that arrived at the front door a few weeks later, also from an anonymous donor.

We were surrounded in Brent Way by a healthy mix of faiths. The Reynoldsons, who were high Anglicans, lived next door on one side of us at Number 65, and the Stranskys, who were Jewish, on the other at Number 69. Eric Reynoldson had been in the merchant navy, and worked for Union Castle Lines in the city, where he found my father a job as a ledger clerk. I visited him in his offices once, and found him sitting up on a high chair writing up bills of lading. It was a quite Dickensian scene, and made a strong impression on me.

Mr. Stransky was a rabbi, and the family was strictly orthodox. We heard them chanting every Friday evening, and my father used to open their mail for them on Saturdays to save them from breaking the Sabbath.

We had a mad spaniel, which my mother used to take for walks with two other dog owners in Brent Way: Mrs. Fransham, who was a Roman Catholic, and Mrs. Booker, who was an atheist. Sometimes I went with them along the cinder track, past the now re-built tennis courts and pavilion, through the gap in the railings, over the stream by a wooden bridge, and up the track that leads between the two halves of the Finchley Golf Course.

The Franshams had lived at Brent Way throughout the war. Their house was one of the closest to the doodlebug that fell on the tennis courts. They had two sons, one of whom was paraplegic. They kept hens on their allotment, and when they went on holiday, we used to look after the hens for them, which involved boiling up potato peelings in a giant pressure cooker and mixing the resultant foul-smelling sludge with meal. They also owned a Pianola, and sometimes I was allowed to go and play on it. When I wrote *The Raging of the Sea*, I modeled my fictional Jannaway family on the Franshams.

Having passed my eleven-plus by rather dubious means, my ambition was now to get into the Navy, and I welcomed every contact I could get with the Senior Service. My father actively encouraged my interest. He taught me the Morse code and introduced me to the bowline, the round turn and two half hitches, and the eye splice. He also made a model of the mast, spars and rigging of a gaff cutter, complete with running rigging, ratlines and even proper blocks with sheaves, which he carved by hand. Each year he took me to the Royal Tournament at Olympia to watch the Royal Navy's Field Gun competition. I read Alan Villiers' *Stormalong* and Armstrong Sperry's *The Boy Who was Afraid*; and began to include in my nightly prayer the line, "O Lord, please help me to get into the Royal Navy."

I was given *A Sailor's Pocket Book* and a monthly subscription to the *Sea Cadet*. I also had a pre-war boys' annual, which contained pictures of boys undergoing naval training at Shotley, near Harwich. Having studied the pictures closely, I decided I would like to join the sea cadets, but my parents didn't think this was a good idea as the sea cadet headquarters was in Southgate, a rather rough area, and they considered sea cadets to be lower class. But they did agree to my joining the sea scouts, and on a wet and windy September evening soon after my eleventh birthday the scoutmaster called in his duffel coat and cycle clips. He called me Captain Oates, which I thought silly and condescending.

Within a few weeks, I had been kitted out with blue shorts, a blue jumper with "Sea Scouts" embroidered in white cotton on the front, a sailor's hat, and a dark green scarf that was threaded through a leather band called a "woggle."

I was very small and skinny for my age and must have looked quite absurd in my Sea Scout outfit. My sisters called me a sea sprout. I cycled up to a chilly hall once a week and did all, or most, of the things that scouts do, like Bob-a-Job Week, winning badges, and playing British Bulldog, an all-against-one fighting game. My parents dutifully attended a parents' night, and in the summer the troop put on an imitation of a field gun display using a handcart that we took to pieces and put together again, after which it was turned into an observation post by sitting the smallest scout (me) on the handle and upending the cart so that I was lifted high in the air.

My membership of the sea scouts came to an end one summer's evening when I was cycling home. I was overtaken by the senior scout, a burly lad called Dave. He swung his racing bike in front of mine, forcing me to stop. He then dismounted and gripped my wrist very firmly indeed and made me walk my bicycle beside his, down to the disused air-raid shelters in the park at the bottom of the hill; and there, among the dirty lavatory paper and torn out pages of men's magazines, he sexually assaulted me.

I was deeply ashamed of what had happened and said nothing to any one. When my scouts' evening came round the following week, I got ready as normal and set off on my bicycle. But I did not go to scouts. Instead, I cycled round and round for nearly an hour before returning home, where my mother remarked that I was back early.

I repeated the performance for several weeks; but one misty evening in October, the scoutmaster turned up in his duffel coat to enquire about my prolonged absence. I kept the truth to myself, saying only that I hadn't felt like going. I was told to go up to my room, and five minutes later the scoutmaster left. I didn't go back to sea scouts after that.

My parents never asked why I had stayed away from sea scouts. Did they have no suspicions whatsoever as to a possible cause? If so, they must have been extremely naïve. But I don't think they were naïve. Perhaps they thought it better to sweep the whole thing under the carpet and pretend it hadn't happened. If so, it was the worst mistake they ever made.

Self-esteem and achievement being intimately linked, my performance at school deteriorated. I didn't have the confidence to invite any school friends back to the house, whose poor state of interior decoration was unchanged, and felt little inclination to work at any subject other than English. But writing compositions was not work as far as I was concerned: it was the only escape available from the awfulness of life at 67 Brent Way.

At Mr. Strong's singing class one afternoon, while singing "As I was going to Strawberry Fair," I became over-enthusiastic and substituted "rifle, rifle, sausages and trifle" for "rifol, rifol, fol-de-riddle-i-do" in the chorus. Only that morning, I had been caught putting soap on the drinking fountain by Jackson, the school handyman. Now, Mr. Strong told me to go and stand outside the headmaster's study. But I funked it and hid myself in the bicycle shed.

I was quickly found out, and brought before the headmaster. Mr. Vogel was a tall, imposing, Oxford man with cheeks like the pouches of a hamster and a habit of scratching his bottom through his grey worsted trousers. He bid me enter his study and close the door behind me. When I had done so, he informed me that he was going to beat me. Feeling as if I were in the middle of a nightmare (beating was very rare at UCS) I bent over a chair and he administered three strokes that were so painful that, in an odd way, they were not painful. When I thanked him, he looked a little embarrassed and said something about not taking any pleasure in what he had done.

That night in the shallow bath I took twice a week, I examined the damage. The discovery of three purple wheals on my bottom caused me more shame than Dave's sexual assault. This was another secret that I was to keep, and reinforced the feeling that I had to be entirely self-reliant and could never expect comfort, support, or love from any living person.

10

A public baptism was held at Oakleigh Hall that summer, at which Susan and Jan were accepted into the communion of the saints. The ceremony took place on a Sunday evening in place of the gospel service. Baptism by immersion always drew a crowd, and was seen by the Brethren as an opportunity to make converts. The hall was packed, curious unbelievers standing at the back to watch the fun. The cover of the baptism tank, over which the communion table stood on Sunday mornings, had been removed and the tank filled with warm water. For half an hour, while Queenie Finch pumped away at the organ, we had a warm-up session of gospel hymn singing. Then Mr. Finch appeared in a pair of angler's waders, followed by Susan, Jan, and my mother, who had been helping them change into old clothes worn over bathing suits.

After we had sat through a Gospel address, during which the speaker explained the meaning of baptism as dying with Christ and rising with him to a newness of life, Mr. Finch stepped down into the baptismal tank and beckoned to Susan, who accepted his hand and descended into the water beside him. When she had borne witness to the fact that she had accepted the Lord Jesus Christ as her Savior, Mr. Finch said, "I baptize thee in the name of the Father, and of the Son, and of the Holy Ghost," and pushed her backwards into the water, immersing her totally before lifting her back up again.

When Susan had retired, dripping and in visible distress, to the hall at the rear, the performance was repeated with Jan and a boy of fifteen; and as each came up out of the water, having symbolically died with Christ and risen again, we sang a chorus that left several of the Sisters in Christ somewhat less than dry-eyed:

> Living he loved me,
> Dying he saved me,
> Rising he carried
> My sins far away.
> Now I am justified,
> Always and ever …

The following Sunday, when my father broke bread at the morning meeting, my sisters took communion for the first time. From that day on, I was the only one in my family (and sometimes in the entire assembly) not in communion. Week after week, I sat bolt upright in my UCS blazer and short grey trousers as first the silver salver with the broken bread passed me by, and then likewise the silver goblet of wine.

I was not old enough to understand what effect this might have on me, but I am old enough now. I was effectively being trained to resist all attempts to follow the crowd and do what was hoped and expected I would do. I was becoming alienated from a family that was itself alienated—by class, by intellect, and by lack of money. I was becoming an outsider in a family of outsiders, which belonged to an exclusive sect, and which saw itself as existing outside worldly society. I know this has marked me, and that I have always had a problem socializing and making friends. But what has been done cannot be undone.

After their baptism, Susan and Jan started attending some of the meetings during the week as well as the three Sunday meetings. The prayer meeting was on Monday, the Youth Fellowship on Wednesday, the Women's Missionary Fellowship (which my mother attended) on Thursday afternoon, the Bible Reading on Thursday evening and, once a month on a Friday, the Oversight meeting, which my father attended.

The Oversight consisted of half a dozen of the elder brethren: Mr. Warner, Mr. Finch, Mr. Henry, Mr. Robinson, Mr. Minto, and Mr. Wheeler. These "elders" met on the first Friday evening of the month to discuss such things as finances and proposals for an extension to Oakleigh Hall. Their function was also, very occasionally, disciplinary. In one case, of which I have close personal knowledge, an intelligent, amusing, and self-confident young woman of thirty ran off to live abroad with a man who was an "unbeliever." When the affair went wrong, she returned home. But she had been excluded from the assembly, and in order to be received back into communion was required to come before the Oversight to acknowledge the error of her ways and be admonished. This effectively broke her spirit: she never fully regained her self-confidence.

My father seldom got back from an Oversight meeting before midnight, and sometimes he would not be home before two or three in the morning. Who knows, perhaps he stopped off for a little light refreshment—or entertainment—on the way home.

I spent as little time as possible at Oakleigh Hall. While the rest of the family took the tube from West Finchley to Totteridge, I cycled to the Sunday morning meeting, usually arriving there before them. After it was over, I would race back to get the potatoes on the boil for Sunday lunch. Sometimes I managed to have urgent homework to do on a Sunday morning and was allowed a respite. But not often: as each Sunday came round, I would try every subtle approach possible to get out of attending, seldom with success. On one such occasion, my mother used a little emotional blackmail. "He gave his life for you, Charles," she said. "Can't you give him just one hour on a Sunday?"

And so it was polish your shoes and put on clean socks and shirt and tie, don your school blazer, and off we go again to obscure readings from Habakkuk or the Book of Hebrews, hymns that left you breathless they were sung so slowly, and Mr. Henry's "we beseech thee" and "in thy loving-kindness" and "in this scene here below."

At home, over the cold roast lamb and mashed potatoes, came the inevitable analysis of the content of the morning meeting, and the assessments of each speaker's contribution. These Sunday lunch discussions were conducted principally by Susan and my parents. Jan made few comments, and I none.

As the weeks and months turned into years, there grew in me a smoldering hatred of the Sunday morning meeting and the Brethren. Though I had never read Hume's *Dialogues Concerning Natural Religion*, it seemed absurd to me to believe that an omnipotent, omniscient and benevolent God should create the human race in the full knowledge that a very large proportion of his rational creatures would, because they had not accepted the Lord Jesus Christ as their Savior, fry for eternity in a hell that "He" must necessarily have knowingly and purposefully created, in advance, to receive them.

Even the New Testament seemed to refute such an extraordinary belief in the text, "As in Adam all die, so in Christ shall all be made alive." If the Bible were true, I reasoned to myself, that sentence must be true, and if that sentence was true, then hell necessarily could not exist and the whole Gospel message with its threat of eternal damnation must be nonsense.

As I came to know the Bible better, I began to realize that for any text on a controversial doctrine there is always another that can be interpreted as contradicting it. On the one hand, we are told, "Come unto me all ye that are heavy laden and I shall give you rest." But we are also warned: "Strait is the gate and narrow is the way, which leadeth unto life and few there be that find it." While there are many texts in the New Testament that exhort us to love one another, and propagate the belief that Christianity is productive of "that peace which the world cannot give," we only have to turn to Luke 12, v. 51-53 to find a contradiction of this view in Jesus' own words to his disciples: "Suppose ye that I am come to give peace on earth? I tell you Nay; but rather division: For from henceforth there shall be five in one house divided, three against two and two against three. The father shall be divided against the son and the son against the father; the mother against the daughter and the daughter against the mother; the mother in law against the daughter in law and the daughter in law against her mother in law."

When I first discovered this passage, I couldn't help comparing Jesus' 'five in one house' to the five of us at 67 Brent Way. Rather than guiding us into all truth, the Holy Spirit seemed to have a strong tendency to sew confusion. I only had to pluck my father's copy of Blair Neatby's *History of the Plymouth Brethren* to see how the sect had been plagued by hair-splitting dissent over the interpretation of Holy Scripture ever since the assembly in Plymouth divided into warring factions under Darby and Newton a hundred years before.

The squabbling continued at Oakleigh Hall. My father seemed to be perpetually engaged in some sort of running battle with one or other of the elders, and burnt the midnight oil writing argumentative letters to them, all of which were well larded with Biblical references.

Meanwhile, from our ivory tower, we looked down upon the vast majority of the human race as being lost to sin, taking pride and comfort in the thought that we were among the Elect of God, and set apart from the world, the flesh, and the Devil.

The ultimate authority for holding these beliefs, observing these doctrines and going along with all this dogma was, as far as I was concerned, my father. He was the pope in our family and we revered his knowledge of Holy Scripture in a most unhealthy way. Sometimes during a mealtime discussion, he would go to the book case, slide open the glass panel and pick out a book, which he would open at the right page and read out the passage or line that he needed.

Most perplexing of all was the change that came over him during his attendance at the morning meeting or when he said Grace before meals. In normal conversation, his delivery was clipped, military, and confident. But when he said Grace, read the Bible, or led the Brethren in prayer at the Breaking of Bread, his whole manner changed to one of fawning supplication: the lieutenant colonel I was proud to call my father was replaced by a quite different sort of person, whose cringing humility I did not admire.

Cycling back from Crusaders one Sunday afternoon, I took an alternative route and was amazed to see him coming the other way in his little Ford Anglia. For a few moments, we were eyeball to eyeball, each shocked and surprised. What he was doing out on his own on a Sunday afternoon I do not know; but I do know that he never referred to our chance encounter.

He was an enigma. I know he was a sensitive, caring, and loving father, but have no memory of his ever giving me a hug or holding my hand. His arrival had put an end to the close relationship I had had with my mother, and his insistence that I stand up straight, abstain from whistling, and spread my butter sparingly on my toast had driven me underground.

But—I don't blame him. All his ambitions had been frustrated, and he had been traumatized by war, first in the bombing and carnage of Boulogne in 1940, and then again during the intensive bombing of Liverpool in 1943.

He was in some respects still at war. He was convinced that the Allied victories over Germany and Japan had marked only a pause in hostilities, and that a far more catastrophic conflict with the Soviet Union, which would inevitably include a nuclear exchange, was imminent. He set great store by the interpretation of Old Testament prophecy, particularly in the books of Ezekiel and Daniel. He saw the restoration of the State of Israel as a sign that we were entering the Last Days before the Lord would come again, and was proud of the fact that he had, before the war, forecast that the Jews would return to the Holy Land.

I was taken and sent on a variety of summer holidays between the ages of eight and fifteen. Our first holiday was by the seaside at Hythe in Kent, where we took rooms in a terraced house overlooking the promenade and the beach and where, in the evenings, my father talked with the landlord about the parlous state of the country. The following year we were given the use of a bungalow at Dymchurch. I fished in the dyke for eels, chopped up stranded jelly fish with my spade, visited a Martello tower, and, rather against my mother's wishes, went to Lympne for the air show, at which a Vampire jet fighter appeared at treetop height, flying at full throttle—followed a second later by the roar of its jet engine.

The Scotts bought an old landing craft after the war, which Uncle Bernard converted to a houseboat. It was anchored in midstream at Burnham-on-Crouch, a few hundred yards to seaward of the Corinthian Yacht Club. We holidayed there on three successive summers, and my father taught me to sail in a sixteen-foot gaff-rigged sloop called *Nab*.

Although my father loved messing about in boats, seamanship was not really his forte and when things went wrong he became very tense. The dinghy had an outboard motor, over which he expended much nervous and physical energy. I think the problem was that he always managed to flood the carburetor. We would drift down on the tide while he pulled the rope, re-wound it, pumped more petrol into the carburetor, and pulled it again, and again, and again—*and again*. In the end, we would give up and row. But if Susan took the oars, the tension rose still further, and the River Crouch echoed to my father's military shouts of "Pull with your right! Pull with your right!" and Susan's tearful, "I *am* pulling with my right!"

He abhorred anything that was in the slightest bit new-fangled. He liked a boat to have a gaff, a boom, and a bowsprit, and looked down on the Bermudan sloop, which he derided as being a "zip fastener" rig. Generally speaking, if there was a new, quick, and easy way to do something, and an old fashioned, laborious, and difficult way, my father would always plump for the latter. The business of rigging the boat always took an age and usually entailed the breaking of one or more of his long, Edwardian fingernails. I suppose it never occurred to him that it might be an idea to clip them before a sailing holiday.

One day we set off early and sailed out past the sand banks into the English Channel. We took two of my sisters' school friends with us. The wind dropped in the afternoon, and it was nearly ten by the time we came creeping in on the tide. So pleased was my father at my ability to sail in a straight line over calm water with the wind steady on the beam that he invited me to steer to our berth alongside another boat. "Just bring us alongside bow to bow," he said. I misunderstood, and started steering the boat so that our bow would point in the opposite direction to the other boat's bow. "Bow to bow!" my father barked, but this only confused me the more. Tension rose. "Bow to bow!" he repeated. "Don't you understand? Bow to bow!" Inevitably, there were tears.

For all that, my father was a kindly man who was desperate for the three of us to make a better fist of life than he had himself. But, for whatever reason—most probably his military service, the loss of his father at age fifteen, and an overbearing mother—he was never able to show much affection to us. There were rare moments when he was able to let go and regain, for a few brief minutes, the person he must have been in his twenties and thirties—the young man who was so full of bounce he was nicknamed "Tigger." On these rare occasions, he would take my mother on his knee and cuddle her, and she would tickle him where she shouldn't and he would put on a funny voice and tell her to be a good girl.

Or, usually while sailing, he might sing one of his army songs. There was "Lloyd George knew my father" and "He was saying goodbye to his horse" and a great favorite that never failed to reduce Susan to shrieks of laughter that went, to the tune of Colonel Bogey:

> Be kind to your web-footed friends
> For a duck may be somebody's mother
> They live in a field or a swamp
> Or any place where it is domp.
> You may think that this is the end—
> Well it is.

Jan's favorite was:

> He's my brother Sylvest (What has he got?)
> He's got forty medals on his chest (Big chest!)
> It takes the army and the navy
> To put the wind up Sylvest—
> (Strong o' de arm, big o' de chest, plenty of
>   room for you and me)
> He's my brother Sylvest ...

As time passed, our preoccupation with spiritual faith seemed to intensify. My mother had never taken us to church while we lived in the Lake District, and I doubt very much that my father attended many religious services while away in the army. Which of them acted as the religiously motivating force, I am not sure. I used to presume that it was my father; but on reflection, I have a feeling that my mother was at least equally responsible for the almost Calvinistic atmosphere that increasingly pervaded our household. Perhaps, unwittingly, they egged each other on. Newly married Christians, take heed.

Unable to afford a new suit, my father took to wearing his old pre-war black morning jacket and pinstripe trousers to the Sunday morning meeting. I used to glance across at him when he was leaning forward in his chair in prayer, his head in his hands, his bushy eyebrows pressed up against his forehead, and wonder what he was saying to God. Perhaps he was begging to be forgiven for all the good times he had while away from his family in India, West Africa, and Norway.

The war, lack of money, the straightjacket of exclusivist religion, and his inability to find gainful and fulfilling employment had all but broken him. In due course, I was to be instrumental in finishing the job.

11

One Saturday afternoon when we were all at home, there was an unexpected knock on the front door. I went to answer it and found a rather glamorous woman in a red coat waiting on the step. "You must be Charles," she said, and came on in without being invited. It was my father's cousin, Molly Prettyjohn.

My parents were courteous to her and entertained her to tea and homemade cookies, but it was obvious that they regarded her with suspicion and disapproval. Even the dog's hackles were up. But I was entranced by her. She was a real woman of the world, the sort you saw in newspapers and magazines. She talked nineteen to the dozen, chain smoked, and left a half-moon of scarlet lipstick on the rim of her teacup.

At length she said she thought she had better be on her way—but could she first go upstairs to powder her nose?

As she left the sitting room, my father whispered to Susan to go with her and not to let her out of her sight. Susan followed her upstairs and found her already at the dressing table in my parents' bedroom.

"It's all right, dear," Molly said. "I can manage quite well on my own."

Susan was embarrassed, and withdrew. A few minutes later, Molly came downstairs and left quickly. When she was gone, Susan admitted that she had left Molly alone in the bedroom, so my mother went upstairs and checked the cut glass pot with a silver lid where she kept a few pieces of jewelry, and discovered that a jade necklace my father had brought back from Egypt was missing.

Molly had been gone about five minutes, and it was a five-minute walk to West Finchley tube station. There was just a chance that we might catch her. My father, sisters, and I set out in hot pursuit. Father went up West Avenue and I up Fursby Avenue. I was sure I would win the race and get to Molly first, but I was wrong: by the time, I arrived at West Finchley tube station, totally out of breath and with a windpipe that felt as if it had been sandpapered, my father had already intercepted Molly.

"Come on, Molly," he said, "hand over." And poor Molly handed over the stolen necklace.

I never expected to see Molly again. But I did.

My last summer term at UCS Junior School approached, and with it the end of year exams. Outwardly, I was a Good Boy. My grey socks were pulled up, my tie well tied, my hair brushed, and my manner attentive and respectful. I stood up straight and I didn't whistle—at least, not when my father was within earshot. I went shopping for my mother and didn't steal very much of the change.

But at school, I was struggling. My mathematics showed signs of chronic carelessness; my Latin and French were average, and now that I had had a change of English master, I was no longer earning the required number of merit points per week to escape the disapproval of my housemaster. I was, furthermore, constantly conscience stricken by my inability to break out of the vice of masturbation, and weighed down with secrets too awful to divulge to a living soul.

Two weeks before the end of term, I was given an hour's detention and lines by Mr. Byrom, the history master. While the electric clock coughed every half-minute on the wall, I sat in the empty classroom and settled down to writing *I must not divert the attention of my neighbour in class* one hundred times.

I came to the end of a page and reached for another sheet from the pile of scrap paper, which Mr. Byrom had provided for the purpose. As I did so, I noticed that the paper smelled of spirit. Curious, I reached for the whole pile and had a close look. It was then that I made an interesting discovery, because at the bottom of the pile of scrap paper I found a sheet upon which, faintly but legibly, was the mirror image of the history examination I was to sit in a week's time.

That evening in the privacy of my six-foot bedroom, which faced across Brent Way and adjoined the bedroom of Jacqueline Reynoldson next door, I held the sheet of paper up to a mirror and studied the questions, and, with the help of the textbook, sought out the answers.

I scored over seventy percent in the history exam and could not help an inward smile when my end of term report arrived and I read Mr. Byrom's comment: "A last minute effort enabled him to achieve a good standard." Much later, it occurred to me that it was just possible that he might, for his own good reasons, have deliberately provided me with a crib. Schoolmasters don't like failures any more than parents or their offspring.

There was, however, a downside to my examination success, because I now had yet another secret to keep. Not only was I a masturbator; not only a boy who had been beaten by the headmaster for putting soap on the drinking fountain, singing "sausages and trifle," and hiding in the bicycle shed; not only one who stole apples down the road, who had played truant from sea scouts, and who was constantly bombarded by sexual fantasies involving the girl from the North London Collegiate School who smiled at me as I cycled past on my way to school—I was also a cheat.

I tried accepting the Lord Jesus as my Savior a couple of times, but it didn't work. I had attended enough Gospel meetings to know that conversion was supposed to bring about a wonderful lifting of the burden of guilt. "Cast all your cares upon Him, for he careth for you," went the text. I tried hard to believe it and prayed earnestly for help to overcome my vice, to be a good boy, to get into UCS senior school, to get into the Navy, to help Mummy more. I wept secretly into my pillow.

But it was no use. The summer holidays had come and there was a Norwegian girl called Isabel who was staying with Heffy and her parents down the road. I fell head-over-heels in love with her, and sought every opportunity to come face to face with her or to catch a glimpse of her looking out from her bedroom window as I went along the cinder track. I think—no, I am certain—that the feeling was mutual; but we were both too young to do anything about it. Even now, fifty-five years later, I sometimes think of her, and am filled with that painful feeling of might-have-been. I wonder what she did in life. She was so beautiful. We spoke only once. I met her coming the other way along the cinder track. We were alone. Our eyes locked. Dry-mouthed, my heart beating wildly, I managed, "Hello." "Hello," she whispered back. But that was all. The next day when I met Heffy on the cinder track she told me that Isabel had returned to Norway, and I never saw her again.

Billy Graham held a gospel mission in Wembley Stadium that year. I've never liked crowds, and I didn't like this one. Billy Graham was like a Greek god with his crinkly flaxen hair brushed back off his forehead to show off his Adonis features to best effect. He held a great floppy Bible that was like a piece of fresh steak in his left hand, and gesticulated with his right. His performance was larded with schmaltz and emotion. He thundered, cajoled, wailed, and prayed. At any moment—*at any moment*—the Lord might come again. Two would be in the fields at the plough; one would be taken, the other left. If we were wise virgins, we would keep our wicks well trimmed: we would pay heed to the text, "Watch and pray, that ye enter not into temptation." If we ignored these clear and solemn warnings it would be, "Depart hence, I never knew you!" on the Day of Judgment, and off we would go to spend an eternity of weeping and wailing and gnashing of teeth.

It was pure salesmanship, with the difference that if you didn't buy the goods, you would fry for eternity. Billy used every rhetorical trick and piece of emotional blackmail to convince us of the need to repent before it was too late. No effort was spared to jerk the tears from us. How could we refuse the Lord Jesus? How could we turn our backs on God's only Son, who suffered, bled, and died for us?

The finale came when, having conversed at some length with the Lord through the public address system, Billy Graham invited all those who had seen the light to come forward, repent, and accept Christ as their savior. Ranged alongside the podium, teams of neatly dressed Christians with second-class diplomas from minor American universities were on hand to counsel the new converts, talk them through their conversion, and explain the after-sales service.

There was a rush to sign up for Jesus. The majority of the converts were girls and young women, for whom Billy Graham's manly charms had evidently proved irresistible; but there were also sad old people who shuffled up as well, some of whom were in tears. The few boys and young men who went up were for the most part clean cut with short hair and blazers. For a fleeting moment, I felt that perhaps I should join them, rather as one is, for an equally fleeting moment, tempted to buy a time-share property. Fortunately, the moment passed.

And then it was home to 67 Brent Way, and a late supper followed by bed; and in the morning it was Sunday, and before getting out of bed I read a portion of the Bible and my Scripture Notes while my father stropped his razor and my mother made porridge and Susan and Jan sang *I would that my love could flow in a single word* in their bedroom, and the smell of burnt toast wafted up from the cluttered kitchen.

12

Our precarious financial situation now drove my father to do the last thing he had hoped or expected to do: apply to the War Office to be taken on as a re-employed officer. His application was successful and he was given a post in AG-7, a War Office department at Stanmore in north-west London, with responsibility for personnel and the post-war reduction in manning levels.

The difficult process of readjusting to civilian life was now reversed. He bought himself the uniform of a retired cavalry officer: a new bowler hat, a new pinstriped suit, and a black umbrella, which he rolled with obsessive care, making sure that the pleats lay flat and tight up the handle, where they were buttoned up with a little band of black elastic.

He was Lieutenant-Colonel James Gidley Wheeler once more. When he came home from the office, he sometimes regaled us with stories about letters he had received from serving soldiers. One was from a sergeant who wanted to know why he was stuck in a frame. Another came from a corporal who believed he had a duck in his head. We found such stories hilariously funny, but now I can't help reflecting that they may have been from men who, like my father, had been traumatized by the horrors of war.

He lived once more in a world of surnames, one of which was Bond—James Bond. I have a feeling that Ian Fleming might have been acquainted with "our" James Bond, who was an exceedingly clean-cut young Major, very ambitious and extremely earnest. He used to give my father a lift to the office each morning. I think it cost James Bond a great deal to bring his shiny black Vauxhall to our lowly suburb. He was a serving officer and as such considered himself my father's superior: he did not like to be kept waiting. This did not irk my father one bit, who was the sort of man who embraced humble servitude, following the New Testament text, "He who would be greatest among you, let him be servant of all."

Twenty-five years later, I bought three acres of orchard land in Portugal from Rita Winsor, who had worked in Turing's code-cracking team at Bletchley Park during the war and later with MI6 as an embassy secretary in Lisbon. Rita had provided visas for W. Somerset Maugham, Ian Fleming, and Malcolm Muggeridge, all of whom acted as agents for the Special Intelligence Service. She once told me that Fleming never put anything in his books that he had not either witnessed or experienced himself. In his autobiography *Chronicles of Wasted Time*, Malcolm Muggeridge described Rita as one of those unsung quartermasters who work behind the scenes to get things done, without whom the war might not have been won. She was a forthright lady who did not suffer fools, and I have a feeling that, if the James Bond who used to give my father a lift to work each morning was the prototype for Fleming's hero, Rita Winsor could very well have been his inspiration for Miss Moneypenny.

Now that my father was in work at the War Office, our finances began to improve. Mother stopped doing night nursing and had the anonymous donation of ten pounds a month cancelled. Though we never discovered who our benefactor was, our chief suspect was my mother's cousin George Rocke, an ex-Grenadier Guards officer awarded the Military Cross during the war.

We started extending hospitality to members of the Meeting by having people back for Sunday lunch, one of whom was Mrs. Tulloch, a war widow from the Shetland Islands, who had worked as a nanny and who acted as housekeeper to a hostel for the elderly in Woodside Park. She had two close friends. One was a cat called Mrs. Keens, the other a tall, blousy woman called Meg Merrilees, who smoked cheroots, smelt of whisky, and had smeary lipstick.

Helen Tulloch had no children and took me on as a substitute son. I swept leaves, picked apples, ate hot bannocks with butter, and drank copious cups of tea with her; and when summer came and my father suggested that she might, for a small remuneration, like to take me on her annual visit to the Shetland Islands to visit her parents, she readily agreed.

We traveled north on the London-to-Glasgow coach, which whisked us at all of thirty-five miles an hour up the A1, through Baldock, Stamford and Peterborough, and on past the Cock o' the North to Carlisle and the Lowlands.

We spent the night with Mrs. Tulloch's cousin and his wife. They lived in a council house and had a thirteen-year-old daughter called Eileen. During our stay, I shared a room with Mrs. Tulloch and Eileen, the ladies in a small double bed, I on a camp bed. I turned in before they did and when they came to bed, having undressed on the landing so as not to wake me; Eileen began telling Mrs. Tulloch, in a stage whisper, about her fears of starting her period.

"Are you awake, Charles?" Mrs. Tulloch asked.

Sex being a taboo subject at home, I was anxious to learn; so I feigned sleep and listened intently while Mrs. Tulloch introduced Eileen to the mysteries, trials, responsibilities, and burdens of becoming a woman.

After a day touring the highlands, Mrs. Tulloch and I took the train to Aberdeen, where we arrived in time to catch the steamer *St. Ninian*. We had oatcakes for tea in the saloon as the steamer pulled out of harbor, and I shared a twin-berth cabin with a dour Shetlander, who was not pleased to be woken at dawn when I saw land out of the porthole and thought we had arrived. "Gang back to thy pit, laddie," he said. "Yon's Fair Isle."

At mid-morning the ship sailed between the Nab and the island of Bressay, and berthed in Lerwick harbor, where a hundred drifters, trawlers, and Norwegian whalers were packed five abreast, and a thousand gulls wheeled and screeched overhead.

The Wisharts, Mrs. Tulloch's parents, lived in a council house on Twageos Road, a five-minute walk from the "auld grey toon" of Lerwick. Mr. Wishart was a retired merchant seaman who had served before the mast in square-rigged ships and on Atlantic convoys during the 1914–18 war. He was a slow-moving, slow-speaking giant with huge hands, a walrus mustache yellowed from chewing tobacco, and a terrible stutter. Mrs. Wishart was a small, thickset, ill-tempered body of few words. Her table manners were non-existent. She never passed anything to anyone or asked for anything to be passed to her. If she wanted the salt and it was out of her reach, she would stand up and grab it—even if it meant lunging to the far end of the table. She never once spoke directly to me, which was probably for the best as she spoke in thick Shetland dialect and I understood little of what she said.

We had porridge for breakfast, Scotch broth—burnt, usually—for the midday meal and herring for supper. To drink there was water, or water.

For four weeks, I became an honorary member of the Twageos Road gang. Its leader was Graham who, being a year or so older than I, introduced me to juvenile delinquency. We hung out by the swings, flirted inadequately with local girls, and when night fell sneaked along the back of the houses in futile hopes of catching a glimpse of something we shouldn't. We stole neaps from the allotments and attempted, with only partial success, to lift the stone off a grave in the churchyard. While these sad little escapades proceeded, Graham confided to me much of his knowledge of girls, and what he claimed to have done with them.

I spent much of my time alone. I liked to walk out to the Nab, the headland at the end of Twageos Road, and watch the gannets diving, the black-backed gulls balancing on up-currents and the seals poking their whiskery heads up to have a look at me. If ever I was late back for lunch, old Mr. Wishart would whistle through his nicotine-stained mustache and mutter, "Headwinds and calms, headwinds and calms." Then we would sit down to eat, and, to her mother's disgust, Mrs. Tulloch would insist upon saying Grace, and the broth would be burnt again, and Mr. Wishart would eat a salted herring, head, tail, bones, and all.

Down at the harbor, rows of chattering women in neck-to-ankle waterproof aprons gutted fish faster than seemed possible: one every three seconds, twenty a minute, a thousand an hour. In went the point of the knife, a clean cut down the belly, and the guts came out in a bloody flash. Two flicks of the hand and the guts went into one barrel and the fish into another—and then reach for the next one, chattering and laughing and exchanging repartee with any man who dared encroach on their domain.

One night I went out on the herring drifter *John West*, a name that is now well known for canned fish. I stood in the dark of the wheelhouse and we tossed, pitched, and wallowed. I was abominably seasick. The skipper ran the echo sounder and found a shoal of herring and the crew went out on the deck in oilskins and paid out upwards of two hundred yards of nets over the bow. And while this went on, the skippers talked endlessly over the radio to other skippers: "John West, John West, John West calling Jessie Sinclair, Jessie Sinclair, Jessie Sinclair …"

Mrs. Tulloch had two younger brothers. Bobby was a giant like his father, very slow of speech, with a stutter that sometimes stopped him speaking for several seconds at a time. The other brother, Jim, worked on the salvage tugs and was immensely strong. He was a fanatic body-builder and could open his four-spring biceps developer to full stretch without any apparent effort.

As with many Shetlanders before the boom of North Sea oil, the Wisharts lived close to the bread line. They kept a peat fire burning day and night, winter and summer. To help out with the housekeeping, Mrs. Tulloch took me on the peat moors to scavenge for sheep's wool left on briars, fences, and stone walls. We took our pickings to a bulk merchant in Lerwick to be weighed, and were pleased to be paid five shillings for the best part of a day's work.

One day we took a bus and went up to see some friends who lived near Sullum Voe. They gave us a warm welcome and we had a meal with them, which consisted of new potatoes, fresh from the earth. They were boiled in a tin bucket and eaten hand to mouth from the same bucket. Nothing else: just tatties. Wonderful!

I was a quiet, introspective, and unassertive child, and the loneliness of the Shetland Islands suited my penchant for solitude. I wandered for hours over peat bogs and along stony beaches, sometimes being dive-bombed by skuas or black-backed seagulls.

The Shetlanders had a language of their own. "How are you?" was "Fu is dhu?" and "a pirrie scar o' tay" was "a little cup of tea." They pronounced w's as q's, so something like "frae quwhere didya get de baldie?" meant "where did you get your hair cut?" and "quwhat like were de puctures?" was an enquiry about a visit to the cinema.

Down by the harbor Graham and I fished for pilticks, and occasionally treated ourselves to three-penny bags of what I vouchsafe were the best potato chips in the world. On my thirteenth birthday I was allowed to make a long distance telephone call to my mother that was more memorable for its novelty and high cost—one shilling and sixpence (about 15 cents) for three minutes—than the "hullo-darling-happy-birthday-are-you-having-a-lovely-time?" conversation. In a curious way, I felt further from home, lonelier, and more homesick after the call than before it. Never visit a dog in kennels until you're ready to take it home.

A week after my birthday we sailed for Aberdeen aboard the *St. Clair*, and I returned to the routine of school, homework, the Sunday morning meeting, and Crusaders.

I went back to the Shetlands for another holiday with Mrs. Tulloch the following summer. Because I had spent so much time on my own the previous year, I was introduced to Charlie Stout, a crofter who lived in a tumbledown stone cottage at the head of Sound, a mile or two from Lerwick. He took me out fishing in the late summer evenings. Whiting and mackerel were in huge abundance—we caught them by the dozen, bringing in upwards of a hundred fish within the space of an hour. We also went flook-sticking. A glass-bottomed box was rigged over the stern and a twelve-foot barbed pole was used to spear flat fish and bring them bleeding and flapping to the surface.

One afternoon when I went round to visit Charlie Stout, I met two girls of my own age, Pamela and Jenny, and we lay on the wind-blown grass on the Ness of Sound and flirted. "Is dhu a boy?" Pamela asked me, and when I said yes, she challenged me to prove it. I refused, but one of the neighbors, a man of forty, who had come out to "play" with us, held me down and was about to provide proof when he suddenly thought better of it. It was not a pleasant moment.

While Pamela was blonde, buxom, and noisy, Jenny was brunette, petite, and shy. We conducted a sort of mute courtship, which consisted largely of standing behind a stone wall and gazing in silence into each other's eyes. "Dhu's aafu' bonny," she whispered to me on my last day. "Quill you write me?"

As the steamer moved away from the quay side of Lerwick harbor I gazed down into Jenny's upturned face with an ache in my heart and a lump in my throat. I was fourteen years old, and I was in love.

13

Now that I was the only member of my family who had not been baptized, I came under increasing pressure to "believe in my heart and confess with my lips" that Jesus had died on the Cross for my sins. Having listened to well over a hundred Gospel sermons, I knew the formula so well that I was confident that I could preach one with no difficulty—and probably more clearly and persuasively than some of our visiting speakers.

First, I would establish that the Bible, as the inspired Word of God, was an infallible guide and as such literally true in every detail from the creation story in the Book of Genesis to the apocalyptic prophesies in the Book of Revelation. Then I would recount the circumstances of the fall—how Eve was tempted by Satan in the guise of a serpent, and Adam was persuaded by Eve to eat the forbidden fruit of the Tree of Good and Evil, so staining the whole human race with Original Sin. Then I would refer to Old Testament passages about the sacrifices ordained to be made by the Children of Israel to atone for their sins, and the prophecies in the Book of Isaiah of a Messiah, a man of sorrows and acquainted with grief, whose sacrifice would end, once and for all, the need to sacrifice animals on altars. Then I would jump forward to AD 33, when Jesus, God-made-Man, enters Jerusalem on the back of a donkey, conducts the Last Supper, dies on the Cross and rises again to conquer death.

Finally, I would explain the choice, open to all, between accepting and rejecting Christ's offer of salvation. To be assured of your place with the saints in heaven, all you had to do was accept Jesus into your heart, confess publicly that you had done so, and die and rise again symbolically with him in the waters of baptism. But if, having heard the gospel message and understood it—and you have now, haven't you?—you choose to reject it and turn away from Christ, then, after the Resurrection of the Dead when the books are opened and you come before the Judgment Seat, gentle Jesus meek and mild will not be so gentle, meek, or mild after all. He will tell you, in modern parlance, to get lost. "Depart hence," he will say. "I never knew you"—and you will be cast into the Lake of Fire, to weep and wail and gnash your teeth for all eternity.

What an unpleasant threat it was—far and away less just or merciful than the story Socrates tells in the "Myth of Er" at the end of Plato's *Republic*, to which the prophecies of the last judgment in the Book of Revelation, written over three hundred years later, bear such uncanny resemblance. At least in Plato's version even the wickedest tyrant or dictator gets a chance to mend his ways, albeit by having to return in a later incarnation as a rat or a snake. But the Christian Gospel presents you with an offer that, if believed, can hardly be refused: eternal bliss with the saints in heaven, or eternal punishment in hell. You're not even allowed the comfort of oblivion.

After my return home from the Shetlands I spent most of my waking hours thinking of Jenny. I had a model yacht that I used to sail on the Leg-of-Mutton pond on Hampstead Heath. To my mother's wry amusement, I painted the name JENNY on the stern.

A week or so later, a letter arrived from my beloved. She enclosed a snapshot of herself: a little girl in short white socks, a gymslip, and white blouse, sitting on the grass outside her grey stone cottage on the windy ridge of the Ness of Sound.

Although I remember nothing of the content of her letter, I do remember that she made her feelings about me plain, and that it brought with it a flood of happiness and excitement that I had never known before.

I had virtually no experience of love. Although my mother kissed me goodbye every day when I set off to school, I don't remember ever being hugged tight by her (or anybody else for that matter) or being told that I was important to her or that she loved me. On the contrary, she had once let slip that my arrival into the world had been a mistake. It was a lighthearted remark, but she never retracted it, and it went deeper than she could possibly have realized. No doubt, both my parents did love me in their own a way, but I don't think ours could possibly have been called a loving family. All the love was saved up for Jesus.

Love, as far as I was concerned, was something more to be sung about than experienced. Inside Oakleigh Hall, love was all over the place. "Love Divine all loves excelling," we sang, and, "How sweet the name of Jesus sounds in a believer's ear." Hymns and New Testament quotations set love on a plane that was certainly beyond my reach and, I believe, out of the reach of all human beings. It was taken for granted that you could treat Jesus as a personal friend—almost a lover—with whom you could have meaningful two-way conversations "along life's narrow way."

Such imaginary love of an imaginary being is not productive of a fulfilled and happy life. It devalues human love and renders sex an unmentionable and undesirable residue, like the tea dregs my mother used to fling down on the coconut matting in the hall to lay the dust.

Sex, as far as I was concerned, was Marilyn Monroe, girls' breasts, masturbation, and songs that went, "You made me love you, I didn't want to do it." Sex was secrecy and fear of eternal punishment. Guilt went hand-in-hand with sex, and the more I found out about it, the more I *did* want to do it.

And now I had this innocent letter from Jenny.

I stole a sheet of my mother's notepaper and, ignoring her oft-voiced advice of "never put pen to paper," went up to my room and set about composing a reply in which I told Jenny how much I thought about her and missed her, declaring my love, and putting several kisses under my name at the end. That done I sealed the envelope, addressed it, and gave it to my mother to post the next day.

But my mother did not post it. She opened it and read it; and the following afternoon took me aside and told me that I was too young to be writing that sort of thing and that it was wrong to say things—whether aloud or in a letter—that one did not sincerely mean. Just because Jenny had written in that way did not mean to say that I should reply in like manner.

It would be too simplistic to say that I felt betrayed. It was more complicated than that. I was in a tide-rip of emotions, pulled one way by my calf love for Jenny and the other by respect for my parents. I knew that what my mother had said was partly true, and I was a little ashamed that she had read what I had written. But I felt deeply wronged all the same.

For the first time I consciously acknowledged to myself that I was unhappy. I hated the unctuous hypocrisy of the Sunday morning meeting at Oakleigh Hall. I loathed having to attend Crusaders every week and sing choruses that claimed that Jesus lived within my heart. Jesus did not live within my heart. If anyone at all lived within my heart, it was the girl with shining brown hair and a shy smile whose eyes I'd gazed into on the Ness of Sound.

One Saturday afternoon I sat on my bed and stared vacantly out of the window. A pianist who had recently lost his wife to cancer was playing a sonata in the house opposite. I put my post office savings book in the inside pocket of my school blazer, went downstairs, wheeled my bicycle out through the front door, and, with my eyes full of tears and my heart full of anger, swung my leg over the crossbar and set out, heading northwards.

It was a windy September afternoon. My intention was to make my way four hundred miles north to Aberdeen, stow away on the *St. Ninian*, and reunite with Jenny. I went up the hill to Ballard's Lane, through Tally Ho, and on to Barnet, where I joined the Great North Road. I knew it well, having traveled up it twice on the coach to Scotland.

It began to rain. I put on the yellow cycling cape I kept rolled up behind the seat and continued on my way. Darkness fell. I was north of Hatfield now and still going strong, with the wind and rain behind me and my yellow oilskin cape acting like a sail to carry me along.

A few miles north of Hatfield, my lights failed.

I dismounted and pulled the bicycle onto the grass bank a yard clear of the wheels of the heavy trucks that thundered past. After cycling for over three hours, I was emotionally and physically drained, and it now dawned on me that my attempted escape was hopeless.

I pushed the bike back along the main road until I came to a garage. There I discovered that the electric lead from the dynamo to the headlight was broken. I asked the man if he had some wire to mend it, which he had, but it cost a shilling and I had no money. Somewhat reluctantly, he agreed to part with a shilling's worth of flex, and allowed me to mend the lights on his forecourt. I said I'd pay him back as soon as possible, but I never did.

I arrived home a little after eight, wheeled my wet bicycle into the hall, and went up to my room. No one remarked on my absence, and I was not welcomed back. From that day to this, nothing was ever said about my abortive attempt to escape.

The next day I did a most shameful thing. I wrote a postcard to Jenny, whose content is burnt so deep into my memory that I remember it verbatim:

> Don't write. I am going to join the Britannia Royal Naval College, Dartmouth.
> Yours sincerely,
> C.H.G. Wheeler.

Fifty years later, in the spring of 2003, I made a trip back to the Shetlands, located "Jenny" (it's not her real name), who still lives on the Ness of Sound, and apologized to her. But, in spite of the current fad of inviting nations to apologize for the sins of previous generations, apologies neither undo the past nor absolve the wrongdoer from the wrong he has done. Whether we like it or not, we become the sort of people we are by doing the sort of things that we do. History provides no left luggage department. Whether as a nation or an individual, we are condemned to hump our baggage around with us.

14

Sitting in the front row at the Sunday morning meeting, on view to every other member of the assembly of saints, I was intensely self-conscious as, week after week, the bread and wine passed me by, and my mother, sisters, and father fell like dominoes into prayer. There were moments when I would look around and realize that I was the only person present with my head up and my eyes open. It was the best possible way of inculcating an independence of mind and obstinate refusal to toe a party line.

Watching my family at prayer in those intense moments after eating a piece of bread and taking a sip of wine, I could never understand why they made such a show of their worship. Why, I used to wonder, was it necessary for my father to lean right forward in his seat and put his nicotine-stained fingers up over his bushy eyebrows? Why, when my sister prayed, did she have to shut her eyes so tightly that her whole expression became contorted? Why could they not simply sit where they were and close their eyes?

Years later when I read *Being and Nothingness*, I discovered the answer to my question in Sartre's example of the waiter in a café who is a little too attentive and who balances his tray too precariously in his hand as he weaves his way between the tables. He is, says Sartre, "playing at being." Christians who make a great show of being bright, keen and jolly—the people you see smiling radiantly for the cameras on televised church services—are doing just that. Sartre calls it *mauvaise foi* or "bad faith."

Because one of the senior boys at Woodside Park Crusaders had taken a shine to me and was following me around, I asked my parents—without telling them the reason why—if I could change to the Finchley Crusaders, and they agreed. A few months after making the change, I was presented with another Crusader Bible for regular attendance, its presentation sticker signed by all four Crusader leaders. I knew very well that I had not earned this Bible by a further hundred Sundays' attendance at Crusaders, but was too naïve to appreciate that I was being groomed for conversion.

The pressure I was under took the subtlest form. It became virtually impossible for me to opt out of the Sunday morning and evening meetings, and I was also being encouraged to take part in Christian events such as games of "podex" (an old English version of baseball) and squashes.

Squashes were socio-religious evenings ("get-togethers") for teenagers, usually held in a wealthy Christian's house. There would be a sandwich supper washed down with watery orange squash or milky coffee, followed by a talk by a bright, keen, and jolly man known as a "youth leader." We "young people" (how I came to detest that expression!) would sit on pile carpet and listen to a handsome young cricketer called David Sheppard give a gospel talk that was peppered with reminiscences of his time as an army chaplain on the Normandy beaches. During one of these gospel pep talks, I made a point of ogling a girl across a short expanse of Wilton, and by gum, she didn't half ogle me back.

Weeks turned into months, and still I refused to come to the Lord. I knew that my time was running out. I knew that my non-conversion was a source of worry to my parents. I think it probable that the brethren were praying for me at the Monday prayer meetings in Oakleigh Hall, and I've no doubt my parents and sisters prayed for my conversion every night. Certainly, I returned the compliment with my nightly, "O Lord please bless Mummy and Daddy and Susan and Jan, and all my friends and relations, and help me to work hard at school, and if it be thy will help me to get into the Royal Navy ...'

It was about this time that my father decided that we should read Bagster's *Daily Light* every morning at breakfast. The *Daily Light* strings Bible texts together to make up a short reading for each day of the year, with pages at the back for special occasions. My parents thought it was probably divinely inspired because its content, like astrological predictions in tabloid newspapers, so often seemed to have direct application to a current crisis. This they saw as proof of Divine intervention, in which they believed unquestioningly.

It's perhaps difficult, today, to understand the mindset of Christians who were so totally committed. They bore misfortune without a grumble, never wavered in their belief in the Lord's loving kindness, and often recounted examples of answers to prayer, whether for guidance to solve a problem, find a lost possession, or even hasten the arrival of a number thirteen bus. The secular version of this sort of superstition is "mind control," by which it is said to be possible to force traffic lights to turn green when one is in a hurry, or find the only available parking space in the center of town.

Any stroke of luck was the Lord's doing; any misfortune was a cross to bear. All hardship, misfortune, illness, poverty, or failure was to be endured cheerfully, in the knowledge that by doing so one stored up treasures in heaven or added a jewel to one's crown.

Far from drawing me into the religious bosom of my family, those morning readings of the *Daily Light* over the porridge and top-of-the-milk only served to increase my impatience. But I was careful to maintain the outward and visible appearance of the good boy I had so often prayed to be tomorrow.

I was in long trousers now, and wore starched collars with my school uniform. My hair was well brushed; my shoes were polished; my knees were seldom dirty. I stood up straight and I didn't whistle because that was the sign of an empty mind. I attended the Sunday morning meeting, joined in the choruses at Crusaders in the afternoon, and in the evening cycled back to Oakleigh Hall for another dose of "O my dear brothers and sisters, will you be among those who go when the Lord comes?"

Eventually, my resistance to the weekly onslaught broke down. One winter evening Mr. Cato, a serving police inspector with a sense of humor and a cockney twang, preached the gospel and did a remarkably good job of it. He spoke succinctly, not too long, and without the verbal hearts and flowers added by so many gospel preachers.

After it was over we sang "Come into my heart Lord Jesus, there is room in my heart for Thee." As I sang those words, I felt a sort of heaviness come over me. I had resisted so very long. Was the Lord deliberately hardening my heart? Was I "kicking against the pricks," as the Apostle Paul had done before he was struck blind on the road to Damascus? Wouldn't it be so much easier to give in?

I cycled home in the dark. When the others arrived back, I went up to talk to my mother in my parents' bedroom.

She had lit the gas fire. A sepia photo of my father, taken before the war, his dark hair brushed straight back off his forehead, stood on the chest of drawers. On the mantelpiece was a selection of his razor blades, each in its cardboard holder, which was marked with the date upon which the blade had been first used. On the bedside table was a clock from the cockpit of a Lancaster bomber, and beside it the black ashtray he had brought back from Norway after the war.

"Mummy," I said, "I accepted the Lord Jesus this evening."

"Oh darling!" she replied, and ran downstairs to break the news to my father.

A frisson of joy went through the house, and for the rest of that evening I was on an emotional knife-edge between laughter and tears. But although we sat down together for our customary Sunday supper of scrambled eggs on toast, to which my father added his usual sprinkle of curry powder, no comment at all was made about my conversion.

I woke up the following morning with the thought that I was now one of the saints, and would be snatched up at the Rapture. But within a few days, I became aware that my conversion experience was all appearance and no reality. I had hoped that accepting the Lord Jesus would end my need to masturbate. But I managed to hold out against the temptation for less than a week, and when I succumbed, the same old feelings of shame and self-hatred returned three-fold and, although I went about with a happy Christian smile on my face, I knew in my heart that my conversion was a sham.

Only a few months before, my mother had advised me never to say or write what I did not mean. Now, on a far more important issue, I had done just that. I was playing at being a Christian. At a time when I was desperately trying to turn myself from a boy into a man, and grappling with the first signs of a late puberty, I had caved in to the emotional blackmail of evangelical Christianity. The knowledge that mine was a pseudo-conversion, and that the apple of my soul was as rotten as ever, served only to alienate me further from my family, and to lower my self-esteem.

For girls, Christian conversion can, perhaps, be seen as a rite of passage on the road to maturity. In giving herself to the Lord, a girl of fifteen becomes a spiritual bride. But with testosterone kicking in, few boys of fourteen want to surrender themselves to anyone, least of all the Lord Jesus.

One Saturday morning, when I was alone in the house, I went to my parents' wardrobe, took out my father's service revolver, loaded it with a single .303 round—the brass-headed type, not one of his dum-dum bullets—and cocked it. I knew that the best way to do it was to put the muzzle in your mouth and fire upwards. It was hard and cold, and tasted of oil. I fingered the trigger for a few seconds, but lost my nerve.

I took the revolver down to the back garden and, after checking that no neighbors were watching, fired it with a massive report towards the tall chestnut trees that grew by the stream beyond the allotments.

I now needed to escape, and the Royal Navy offered an obvious route. I asked my mother to ask my father (I never dared approach him directly on any subject) to send for the application forms for the entrance examinations to the Royal Naval College, Dartmouth.

Judging from the carbon copy of a letter to my headmaster, which I came across years later in my father's papers, my parents were not at all happy at the thought of my joining the Navy, though I daresay my father took vicarious pleasure in the prospect of seeing his son attempting what he had longed to achieve forty years before. That they never voiced their concern to me is a measure of the lack of communication between us: I had no idea that I was going against their wishes. Perhaps my father already sensed that I was in a state of suppressed rebellion. In a letter to Mr. Walton, my headmaster, he wrote:

> My wife and I have discussed it from every angle that seems relevant, and we are both of the opinion that the only thing is to let him have his try. What I am afraid of is that, if he were not allowed to do it, he might take an awkward turn through feeling frustrated. I did myself! [...] Personally, I am nursing the hope that the Selection Board may spot those streaks in his temperament which might make a Service life uncongenial, but if he were to get through, we could only wish him the best of luck and give him all the backing we have.

The application form had to be completed in my own handwriting. With my father hovering anxiously behind me, I became nervous and made a mess of the front page. This caused him much tension and impatience. But the fact that I'd smudged the address and had two shots at spelling "January" didn't affect the outcome, and confirmation was received that I was to sit the entrance examination in March 1954 for entry to Dartmouth in September of that year.

15

On June 2, 1953, my sisters and I rose at three in the morning and went by tube to Piccadilly, where we joined the throng to watch the Coronation procession. We were out in the world, mixing with the hoi polloi. Young men were whistling at girls across the road, and all around us there was repartee and an atmosphere of London cheerfulness. People shared sandwiches and asked each other about their mothers-in-law. Policemen were friendly and unarmed. Forward young women who wore too much lipstick were flirting with the soldiers lining the route. When a young cavalry officer trotted past on a gleaming horse, he was greeted with cheers and catcalls that turned his neck scarlet.

We waited, and waited. Copies of the *Daily Express* were handed round, on the front page of which was a photograph of Sherpa Tensing standing on the top of Mount Everest. Well, of course, I thought. One took it for granted that Britain would be first to do that, just as Roger Bannister had been first to run a mile in under four minutes, and Peter Twiss held the world air speed record. We were British. We were always first to do everything. This was the dawn of a new Elizabethan age.

We had been waiting six hours by the time the coronation procession came past. All the Commonwealth countries were represented, and each brought along a company of warriors to march ahead of their representative. New Zealanders, Canadians, Pakistanis, Sikhs, Ghurkas, and Australians marched proudly by. Eventually we heard a crescendo of cheering in the distance and knew that our new Queen must be approaching. The cheers became louder and louder—until suddenly there she was, reclining in an open carriage, showing white teeth in a wide, delighted smile, waving for all she was worth, a garland about her neck and a flower in her hair. The Queen of Tonga was undoubtedly the star of the show.

There were contingents from every uniformed service. The firemen, the police, the ATS, the WAAFS, and the WRNS—in black stockings and perfectly in step—came marching past. Then came the Royal Air Force, and after them the naval contingent in white gaiters and white belts. Finally, the jingle of harness announced the cavalry of the Household Division.

Riding in a golden carriage, the new Queen, dressed in ermine and weighed down by the priceless crown on her head, trundled majestically by. I was too old to be pushed to the front with the children, but too small to see much over the shoulders of the crowd, so I only caught a brief glimpse of her as she went by—and I was so overawed that I forgot to cheer.

Why my parents did not choose to come with us to watch the coronation procession I don't know. Instead, we made a rendezvous with them in London that evening. But, within minutes of doing so, an argument ensued over whether we should go to Buckingham Palace to see the royal family come onto the balcony, or to the Thames Embankment to watch the fireworks. As a result of this disagreement, we failed to get to Buckingham Palace and also failed to see more than a glimpse of the fireworks. The only thing of interest that I saw was a guardsman throwing up against the statue of Boadicea by Westminster Bridge. (We didn't know her name was Boudicca in those days.)

That family squabble on an evening when the whole of the rest of London was celebrating became for me symbolic of our inability to cope with, or live in, the world. We were different and we always had to *be* different. We did not know how to relax, join in, be one with the crowd, and enjoy the collective fun and celebration of the day. We stood aloof from all that.

This otherworldly refusal to be one with the rest of humanity and accept that usually, if not always, the majority gets it right was, perhaps, my father's greatest failing. It rubbed off on all of us except my mother, whose natural optimism, humor and commonsense provided a much-needed antidote to the underlying tension that droned and throbbed constantly in the background of our lives.

The day ended on a muted note. While London frolicked the night away, we caught the tube home to West Finchley, walked down Fursby Avenue and along to 67 Brent Way, and then it was a plate of porridge, a cup of tea, and bed.

A few days after the Coronation I went down to Portsmouth and boarded an Admiralty paddlewheel tug, which took me, along with a crowd of other schoolboys, up and down the lines of warships anchored in the Solent for the Spithead Review.

I was surprised and disappointed, in a jingoistic way, at the lack of British battleships, there being only one present, HMS *Vanguard*. I was also outraged that foreign ships—particularly the Russian cruiser *Sverdlov*—should be present. It seemed to me that the ships of foreign navies had no right to be present at what was a British celebration, and I couldn't help feeling that they had been invited to make up numbers—to put, as it were, bums on seats.

The largest ship present was the aircraft carrier HMS *Eagle*. I looked at her with disdain, having inherited my father's suspicion of aviation, not for a moment imagining that I might one day fly aircraft off and onto her deck.

For my fifteenth birthday, I was given a Coronation edition of the *Daily Light*. Bound in powder blue mock leather, with "E II R" embossed in gold on the cover, it smelled of fish glue. But although I set it with my Bible and Scripture Notes on the windowsill by my bed to give my mother the impression that I read it every morning, I never did. I didn't like it. It represented for me all the timidity, humility, and self-negation that I now sought to renounce.

All I longed for was to be able to turn my back on my family, the Sunday Morning Meeting, Crusaders, and the Gospel, and to escape into the real world—the world I had briefly glimpsed in the coronation crowds.

16

Pretending to be something that you are not is a self-damaging thing to do. While it may seem easier to copy a role model or stereotype, the more we do it, the more angst we suffer. I did not realize this in my teens, though I was uncomfortably aware of the dichotomy between the outward appearance I presented to the world and the inner reality of the person I was becoming.

To my family I was a reserved boy, small for my age, who had accepted the Lord Jesus and who would, sooner or later, cement his membership of the community of saints by asking for baptism. To my school friends I was a nonentity: a face in a blazer with a Crusader badge in the lapel. To myself I was someone who was full of deceits, masturbated frequently, stole apples, short-changed my mother when I went shopping for her, and was deeply troubled about the false façade I presented to the world.

When I was alone I sometimes sang to myself a current hit, whose lack of subjunctive offended the pompous little grammarian in me that went:

> I wish I was an apple on a tree,
> I wish I was an apple on a tree!
> If I was an apple on a tree,
> A girl might take a bite of me—
> I wish I was an apple on a tree!

At school, I was in the Remove with Mr. Terry, a bald, cadaverous academic who reminded me of Chalky, the schoolmaster of Giles's cartoons. Under Mr. Terry's (and later Mr. Morley's) eye we translated passages from Aristophanes' *The Birds* and Virgil's *Aeneid*, and learnt about ablative absolutes, pluperfect subjunctives, and Greek irregular verbs in the form *smoko, smoxo, leleitepipa, puphmai*.

We also read some of the *Five Dialogues* of Plato. The passage in the *Phaedo* about the last hours of Socrates brought tears to my eyes, and I could not help seeing the similarity between Socrates' view of the afterlife and that of the Christian gospel. Fifty years later, when I studied ancient philosophy at Durham, I became convinced that the Christian religion finds its roots in Hellenistic myths and legend, and is little more than neo-Platonism, with details added to fit in with Messianic prophecies of the Torah. The dialogues and letters of Plato have echoes in the epistles of St. Paul, who, like the Stoic Chrysippus, came from Tarsus; while the similarity between the story of Orpheus and that of Jesus is particularly striking, as both tell of a charismatic young man who descends into hell, rises from the dead, ascends to heaven, and is worshiped as a god.

When the syllabus for the Dartmouth entrance exams arrived, I embarked on the English Literature reading list with enthusiasm. I read Pope's *The Rape of the Lock*, Shaw's *Arms and the Man*, Conrad's *The Nigger of the Narcissus*, Hardy's *Under the Greenwood Tree*, Stevenson's *Travels with a Donkey*, Kipling's *Captain's Courageous*, and Dickens' *Nicholas Nickleby*.

These and other set books ignited my interest in English Literature. I fell in love with the heroines of Hardy's novels and through them slaked, in part, my raging thirst for romance. Stevenson's tragic short story *Olalla*, which was not on the Dartmouth reading list, touched me deeply; and I thrilled to the rustle of silk as the gown fell to the floor in Keats' *The Eve of St. Agnes*.

When the UCS library sold off some of its stock, I used the money I earned from chopping wood for Mr. Manley to buy up works by Hardy, Conrad, Kipling, and Stevenson. Hours that should have been spent on mathematics or science were spent in the school library, sitting on a polished oak windowsill, my knees drawn up, plodding along with Stevenson and Modestine in the Cevennes, reefing topsails aboard the *Narcissus*, or weeping over Hardy's ironic tragedies.

Sometimes I would pause and look up from my book, with its oak-leaf emblem and school motto—*paulatim sed firmiter*—on the spine, and, pushing a finger through the hole in my trouser pocket, imagine myself running through a bluebell wood with a girl in frothy white muslin. We come to a grassy bank and lie down side by side. I look into her eyes. She takes my hand and puts it to her breast and—

Because I believed that no one who indulged in self-abuse could have the remotest chance of becoming a naval officer, I resolved for the nth time never to do so again. Something had to be done. I desperately needed someone in whom I could confide, but there was no one. My sisters looked down on me from hilltops of condescension. To them I was a "pinhead," a "sea sprout," or a "mercenary little beast." And I had so many secrets from my parents that I felt unable to confide in either of them.

One day I took pen and paper and wrote down a brief litany of my sins. I folded up this written confession and put it in an empty Ovaltine tablet tin, which I buried under bushes on the banks of the stream below the allotments. But a week later one of the sixth-form athletic heroes at UCS accosted me on a Saturday morning when I was out on my bicycle, and revealed that he and his friends had unearthed my miserable little confession and had had a good laugh about it.

My determination to join the Navy steadily increased. I loved everything to do with ships and the sea, though my idealized perception of what it would be like to be in the Navy was far distant from the reality, as it was only a few years since I had abandoned the hope of sailing before the mast aboard a tea clipper with topgallants set, homeward bound from Shanghai. Aware of my rose-tinted view, my father used his contacts in the War Office to arrange a visit to a modern destroyer, HMS *Daring*, which was in the final stage of being built at the Royal Dockyard, Portsmouth.

Father and son, JG and CG, the upright military man and his fresh-faced son in a grey flannel suit, traveled down to Portsmouth harbor by train and walked briskly along The Hard, past the Keppel's Head and Gieves Naval Tailors, and on through the main dockyard gates, under cranes, over caissons, along quays to a dry dock at the bottom of which, like a patient on the operating table, lay a very futuristic looking ship with two bulky gun turrets on the bow, an array of radio and radar aerials on the mast, twin anti-aircraft guns behind the funnel, and antisubmarine mortars poking up from the stern.

Escorted by Engineer Captain Spooner, we descended into an inferno of pneumatic hammers, oxy-acetylene welders, and high-speed drills. We picked our way over massive black cables that snaked along the deck and, stepping over the high coaming of a watertight door, walked between decks, inhaling toxic fumes and asbestos dust on our way.

My father had, in his oblique and tentative way, suggested to me that a career in the Foreign Office might be worth considering, and had given me Arthur Grimble's *A Pattern of Islands* to fire my enthusiasm for the Colonial Service. I daresay he hoped that rubbing shoulders with grease-smeared dockyard workers and foul-mouthed naval ratings might persuade me to abandon my naval ambitions, stay on at University College School, read Classics at Oxford, and seek a career as a diplomat. But I was not to be put off. All that our visit to HMS *Daring* achieved was to confirm that I had no wish to join the engineering branch of the

Royal Navy. There would be no purple cloth between the rings of gold lace on *my* sleeve. It was to be the executive branch or nothing.

Having extracted ourselves from HMS *Daring*, we were entertained by Captain Spooner in the smoke-filled wardroom bar in the Royal Naval Barracks, where I tasted warm beer for the first time. I didn't much like it; nor did I much admire the booming, boozy bonhomie of the naval officers in the bar, few of whom seemed to be gentlemen and none of whom seemed to be possessed of any culture or interesting conversation.

Did my father glance in my direction, hopeful that these awful people might discourage me? Probably.

Surrounded by murals of famous sea battles and waited on by white-coated naval pensioners, we lunched on mulligatawny soup, braised oxtail, and apple pie. After a small cup of inferior coffee in an anteroom where lieutenants and lieutenant commanders snoozed behind copies of the *Daily Chronicle*, we made our way to Portsmouth station and traveled back by rail and tube to 67 Brent Way.

My father was an old-fashioned gentleman, a species that is now almost extinct. He was the sort of person who would give you the coat off his back, and he put the welfare and safety of his family above all else. He taught me manners: to raise my hat to ladies, stand up when one entered the room, walk on the outside of a lady to prevent the mud from the wheels of carriages splashing her gown, always to ask her permission to smoke, never to block an exit or doorway, always to think of other people and never to leave a telephone to ring unanswered.

I see in him the epitome of Kierkegaard's knight of faith in *Fear and Trembling*. His gruff military manner, his honesty, kindness, courtesy, stoic optimism, and humor were exceptional. But behind the gentlemanly good nature, there was about him a certain sad wistfulness. Having failed to get into the Navy, having failed as a writer, having never been to university, and having had a promising army career cut short by a possessive and demanding mother, all his ambitions—as cavalryman, playwright, publisher, engineer, and businessman—had been frustrated.

He was a man whose potential far exceeded his life achievements. The cause of this was, I have no doubt, the restrictive chains of what Nietzsche calls "Socratism," by which he means the self-effacement, humility, meekness, and poverty of spirit advocated in Christ's Sermon on the Mount. Inside him, constantly but unsuccessfully struggling to get out, was a brave, devil-may-care, Dionysian, artistic existentialist. I daresay that, at some moment of danger during the war, he promised God that if he survived he would dedicate the remainder of his life to Christ.

It was his own thwarted ambition and lack of success in life that must have motivated him to give me every possible encouragement to follow my star. He made no secret of the fact that he was proud of me, particularly the classical education I was receiving at UCS. Although I feared him and was unable to confide in him, I also loved, admired, and respected him with all my heart.

The great tragedy of our relationship lay in the fact that he never seemed to appreciate what a huge influence he could have been on me if only he had tried. Ours was undoubtedly an oedipal relationship: we competed for the attention and love of my mother. Perhaps this was another factor in the strange formality of our relationship, which, by the time I was fourteen, had led me to start calling him "Sir." If only, the first time I called him that, he had taken my hands in his and told me that I should never call him such a thing, that he was my father, that he loved me, and that I could tell him anything and everything without fear of his ever betraying my trust.

But he was never able to break down the emotional barrier between us, or speak openly about the difficulties every boy faces of growing to manhood. It was not his fault, and I do not blame him. It was the fundamentalist religion in which he had been brought up, and which he and my mother handed on to us three children that blighted our lives.

17

The Dartmouth entrance exams were held in March 1954 at Queen Anne's Mansions, close to the Science Museum in South Kensington. For the week of the exams, I stayed with Constance White, a close friend of my mother's and wife of the Harley Street psychiatrist and author, Dr. Ernest White. They lived at 13, Roland Gardens, a five-minute walk from South Kensington tube station.

Auntie Con was a warm, loving Mrs. Do-as-you-would-be-done-by. She had inner jollity and a deep-voiced laugh that was infectious. Her son John converted to Catholicism, married a Catholic, and became a professor at Newcastle University. The news of his conversion was a great shock to my parents who, I believe, had nursed hopes that Susan and he might one day marry. They viewed his conversion to Catholicism as a great tragedy. For my part, I liked and admired him, and his conversion opened up for me the possibility of breaking away from the Brethren. If such an admirable and intelligent person as John White could make so radical a change, perhaps I could as well.

I felt that I was walking with destiny now. On my way to the examinations hall each morning, I muttered my exam number, "nineteen, double one, four seven" in much the same way as I had chanted "e-n-o-u-g-h" or "C-h-a-r-l-e-s" to myself on the way to school ten years before.

Of over six hundred who sat the exam, I came twenty-seventh. However, my father was informed that I had failed the medical on account of excessive level of albumen in my urine. The cause was put down not to physical malfunction so much as inner tension and anxiety. My father appealed against the decision and I was required to spend a day and a night in the London Hospital, where I was injected with a dye that turned my urine an interesting shade of magenta.

Having passed the medical on appeal, I was called for interview, and traveled by train to Dartmouth for the occasion. My batch of nine arrived at the college late in the evening, and after watery cocoa and ship's biscuits, we turned in for the night in one of the dormitories. Close to where we assembled the following morning, a roof was being re-tarred. To this day when I smell hot tar, I think of Dartmouth and my day at the Admiralty Interview Board.

The Board consisted of the president, Rear Admiral Jellico, in tweeds and quiet tie, a pipe-smoking engineer captain, a smooth looking supply and secretariat captain, an executive captain with his head in a bandage (he'd dived into the shallow end of the college swimming pool the previous day), a rather sad headmaster who said very little, and an anemic looking psychologist in a brown lounge suit.

We spent the morning down in the gym at Sandquay by the River Dart. Each candidate had to take charge of the rest in completing an evolution of some sort. My task was to transfer the members of the team, together with an empty oil drum, across an imaginary chasm using only a plank and a single climbing rope dangled out of reach over the center of the chasm.

The problem was set up in our absence and I was given a minute to think out how to use the team to tackle it. We had been told that we could make use of any of the equipment on view. Seeing that there were other climbing ropes that had been pulled to the side of the gym and secured to concrete blocks, I decided that the best way of transferring the oil drum would be to untie two of these ropes, one on either side of the gym, attach them to either end of the oil drum and make a swing, upon which each member of the team could swing across the chasm.

The chief petty officer blew his whistle to start the evolution.

"Right," I said, in an authoritative, albeit unbroken, voice. "We'll untie that rope there and that rope there—"

"No you won't!" barked the executive captain. "That's not allowed!"

This took the wind out of my sails. I thought quickly and came up with an alternative plan, which I began to explain, when one of my fellow candidates effectively took over the show, so that by the end of the evolution I was convinced that I had failed the interview.

After a stand easy break with more watery cocoa and ship's biscuits, came one-to-one interviews with the engineer captain and the psychologist. The engineer captain was an affable man with a ruddy complexion and eyebrows that were almost as bushy as my father's. He sucked at his pipe and asked me about my holidays in the Shetlands. I told him about my night out in a herring drifter. He looked at me with a twinkle in his eye and asked, "Notice anything about Shetland women, did you?" "Yes, sir," I replied. "They have beards." He laughed and sent me on my way.

The psychologist sat sideways at a desk, opened the bottom drawer, and put his unpolished brown shoes into it. There followed a lengthy silence that reminded me of the beginning of the Sunday Morning Meeting at Oakleigh Hall.

"Any trouble at home?" he asked.

"No sir."

"Are you sure you really want to join the Navy?"

"Yes sir."

He nodded to himself for several seconds, reached for my file, looked at it for a few seconds, threw it back onto the desk, and said, with a despondent sigh, "All right. You can go."

Our batch of nine was then assembled to give short talks, delivered to the Board. We had a choice of three subjects and were given five minutes to prepare. My choice of subjects was between Satellite Towns, Field Sports, and Jazz. I didn't know what satellite towns or field sports were, so I picked Jazz, and launched into a diatribe against it, during which I said very little that made any sense at all. By the time the executive captain tapped his pencil on the table to tell me to stop, I was breathless and the members of the Board were looking decidedly glum.

There followed a debate on the question, "Is the bombing of enemy hospital ships morally permissible in time of war?" Brian Wright, an immaculate boy whose way of speaking reminded me of Malcolm Muggeridge (and who in later life became secretary to the Lord Mayor of London) argued, quoting Clausewitz, that there could be no limiting the horrors of war by the imposition of rules. I took the opposing view that the question was itself an outrage and should not even have been raised in the first place. Perhaps I scored a point or two there; but when the interview marks were published, B.R. Wright was ahead of C.H.G. Wheeler.

The final event was an interview by the entire Board. I sat on one side of a long table and they sat on the other. They asked me where I would have chosen to serve, had I been in the Navy during the war. I had read a book about the war in the Western Mediterranean and replied, "Cruisers, sir. Western Mediterranean."

"Why?" asked the Executive captain.

I shrugged and said, "Bravado, I suppose."

The headmaster spoke for the first time. "What books do you like reading, Wheeler?"

I said that my favorite authors were Thomas Hardy and Robert Louis Stevenson.

"Which of Hardy's books have you read?"

"Well—*Under the Greenwood Tree. A Pair of Blue Eyes. Two on a Tower.*"

"And Stevenson?"

"*Treasure Island*, *Kidnapped*, *Ebb Tide*, *The Wrong Box*, and … *Prince Otto*."

The headmaster stared hard at me. I wondered if he could hear my heart thundering in my chest. I had found *Prince Otto* very boring and had abandoned it after the first few pages. All he had to do was ask me what it was about and I would be caught in the lie. But he didn't, and I wasn't.

A few weeks later, I received a letter with ON HER MAJESTY'S SERVICE on the envelope, which started:

> Sir,
>
> I am commanded by My Lords Commissioners of the Admiralty to enclose a table of the results of the recent competition for the entry of Naval Cadets at the age of 16, and to inform you that you have been appointed as a Naval Cadet (Executive) to H.M.S. Dartmouth for the Britannia Royal Naval College, Dartmouth, to enter in September, 1954 …

Of the original six hundred candidates, thirty-six were selected. I was in ninth position.

"Give the boy a bag of nuts!" my father said when he heard the news. I would have preferred a warm handshake and a hearty congratulation. A big hug would have been even better, but the Wheeler family didn't do hugs.

At the end of my last term at UCS, the headmaster wrote to my father:

> Dear Colonel Wheeler,
>
> I have always been selfishly afraid that Charles would get into Dartmouth first time and you know how sincerely we mean it when we say we are sorry to lose him. I do not doubt for a moment that in the examinations he will have produced an even row of good results.
>
> Since hearing about the slight obstacle he had in the medical way to get accepted for the Navy I have come to the conclusion that the inaccuracy that masters still complain of is really due to a well-controlled over-anxiety. So perhaps we need to advise him not to be more careful checking his work but to be a bit more reckless at the start. Naval training I should say is the best possible way of producing the right kind of recklessness.
>
> Yours sincerely,
> C.S. Walton

A week or two later, when my uniform arrived from Gieves, the naval tailors, the enormity of what had happened began to dawn on me and my family. We gathered in the cluttered front room. There were gasps as my brass-buttoned reefer burst forth from its tissue paper wrapping; the uniform cap badge, with its embroidered crown in gold thread, its red velvet, silver anchor, and golden leaves, was particularly admired.

"They've poached your egg nicely," my father commented. Poor man! I think he was green with envy.

Something mysterious was happening, and I was at the center of it. From my earliest years, I had been connected firmly to my family and protected from the outside world of authority and power. The arrival of this uniform marked the first stage of my breaking away from the world of Oakleigh Hall, Crusaders, and the Gospel.

I went up to my room to change into my new uniform. I put studs in the stiff white collar and knotted the black tie. I put on the fine serge trousers, the black socks, and black shoes. I donned the reefer jacket with its single button and white twist on each lapel, and buttoned the four brass buttons; then, with my cap with its glowing cap badge under my arm, I went out to the little back garden and stood by the apple tree and the broken down coal shed for my mother to take a snap with her Kodak box camera.

On my last Sunday as a civilian, I attended the morning meeting in my uniform, where I was given a cool reception from the Brethren. I had for some time felt like a spy in their midst. Now, my cover was blown.

"It'll be half a crown to talk to you now," Mr. Henry observed dryly.

The day finally arrived: September 14, 1954. I put on my uniform, packed my new naval grip, and walked self-consciously with my parents up Fursby Avenue to West Finchley tube station.

We didn't say much in the tube. I was in a daze, and I think my parents, especially my mother, were in emotional turmoil. I was to catch the midday train from Paddington. We arrived half an hour early and hung about on the platform, keeping separate—of course!—from other little groups of parents, sisters, and brothers escorting naval cadets, all of whom looked much older and more mature than I.

The time came to say goodbye. There was a sort of dread inside me. I didn't kiss my mother, nor did I shake my father by the hand. There was no emotional farewell: no hug, no kiss, no sniff, and no damp handkerchief. I picked up the Admiralty issue officer's grip with my initials on it, turned away from them, walked down the platform, and entered a compartment with three other cadets. As the train moved off, I saw my old grey parents looking in at me: my father very erect, my mother keeping back tears.

I didn't wave. Nor did they.

18

I described life as a cadet at Dartmouth in *The Raging of the Sea*. Coming as I did from a day school and an evangelical background, it was not easy to adjust to the gung-ho, Spartan discipline of cold baths, cross-country runs, and beatings for the smallest offence. It might have been easier had I felt able to rely on my parents for moral support. But I did not. The words of *The Miller's Song* still applied. My first three months at Dartmouth served only to intensify my sense of solitude and separation.

In leaving home and joining the Navy, I had exchanged one sort of fundamentalism for another. The Royal Navy was to naval cadets as Christianity was to the Brethren. Both were elitist and authoritarian. Many had been called but few chosen. To be a committed Christian, you had to believe in your heart and confess your faith with your lips. To be a committed naval officer, ditto, ditto, ditto. Just as my mother's eyes would light up when she spoke of the Last Day, when we would be caught up into the clouds and go to be forever with the Lord, so would the eyes of naval officers light up when glasses were raised to the "immortal memory" of Lord Nelson.

Though I was physically at home for my three weeks of leave after my first term, I was not emotionally at home, for the simple reason that I had no emotional home. This was a time when I was caught in cross-currents, unaware of what was happening to me, confused by the conflicting values of my family and the Navy, fearful of failing to stay the course, dismayed by the ethic of violence at Dartmouth, and still self-conscious about my lack of physical maturity. I had no sense of affinity or kinship with any person or organization. I did not belong anywhere: not in the Navy, not in the Brethren, not at 67 Brent Way, and not at Dartmouth in Grenville House.

In the course of my first Christmas leave, I became much more aware of the contradictions and inconsistencies of my parents' social, political, and religious attitudes. One of these lay in their attitude to wealth or worldly success. Calling someone "well-to-do" or "comfortably off" was code for saying that they were "of the world" and could not be true Christians, it being more difficult for a rich man to enter the kingdom of heaven than for a camel to pass through the eye of a needle; and yet my father, who was convinced that he could make a killing on the stock market without the assistance of a stock broker, spent hours every evening in the front room in a haze of cigarette smoke analyzing what my mother referred to as his "shocks and stares."

Although my parents advocated withdrawing from the world, each held attitudes that were not consistent with doing so. My mother spoke nostalgically of her childhood memories at The Croft in Mumbles, a household served by a dozen or more cooks, table maids, laundry maids, and gardeners. My father read the Tory press and held xenophobic views about the superiority of the sons of Japheth over the sons of Ham. When a general election came along and every other front window in Brent Way carried a political poster, we never put one up in ours, because to do so would have been an admission that we were, after all, concerned about which party should form a government. And yet we *were* concerned: my parents abhorred socialism and the Trade Union Movement, and never failed to vote Conservative.

There were other contradictions. They admired success and liked to be able to speak of an acquaintance or relation who had secured an "absolutely top job"—but at the same time held that worldly success was not something to which a Christian should aspire. The Brethren did not approve of drinking or smoking—yet my father kept a bottle of sherry in the sideboard and smoked at least twenty cigarettes a day, which he hand-rolled in a patent cigarette maker, taking pride in the quality of the finished article. Women were not supposed to adorn themselves with jewelry, but away from the disapproving eyes of the elder Brethren, my mother sometimes wore the jade necklace Molly tried to steal. We refused to own a telephone, but for many years presumed upon our neighbor's generosity by popping in to use theirs. We admired the royal family and believed in the British Empire, but we doubted whether any member of the royal family would go to be with the Lord at the last trump.

My mother's side of the family were, for the most part, missionaries in Africa, and we sided with the poor and lowly—and yet we mourned the demise of the British Empire, regarded "natives" as inferior to white men, and blamed Mountbatten and the Labor Party for losing India. Winston Churchill was a great man, yes, but our admiration for him was mitigated by the fact that we did not believe that he had accepted the Lord Jesus as his Savior.

When my father prayed at the Sunday morning meeting, he often referred, in a manner that I thought unnecessarily humble, to the Lord's loving kindness, but outside Oakleigh Hall, he was very much the lieutenant colonel in his manner, his dress, and his conversation. The last line of the Book of Revelation, "Even so, come Lord Jesus" was one of his favorite texts; and yet, although he looked forward to the Last Day, he harbored fears about a future war between the Soviet Union and the West, which, if it happened, would herald the end of the world and the beginning of the prophesied thousand-year rule of Satan. He even went so far as to confide to me that he looked forward to the invention of a mini-atomic bomb the size of a hand grenade, which he believed would make an ideal weapon for Britain to use against a Soviet invasion.

These strange contradictions, coupled with an obsession with Old Testament prophecy, occupied so much of my father's thoughts that there was little room left for the warm, carefree, loving enjoyment of life that should be (but seldom is, in my experience) present in a family that regards itself as devoutly Christian.

Today, in an age when everyone hugs everyone else, it is perhaps difficult to imagine a world entirely devoid of hugs; but that was what my world was like. Both at home and in the Royal Navy, I was led to believe that it was of overriding importance that no living person should ever suspect that I might be subject to any sort of human emotion. On the rare occasions when I cried, I was careful to do so in private, and developed the trick of blinking rapidly to disperse any tears that might have the effrontery to come to my eyes. So, by the time I went back to start my second term at Dartmouth, I was adept at suppressing any tendency to openness about my personal feelings, and when I boarded the train at Paddington, no one knew that I did so with a feeling of intense dread.

I passed out as a cadet a month before my eighteenth birthday in July 1956. My parents came down to Dartmouth for the occasion, but Colonel Nasser had nationalized the Suez Canal and my father was recalled to the War Office at short notice to do his bit in calling up reserves for the landings in Egypt. So, while I marched past the saluting base to the drumbeat of the band of the Royal Marines playing *Hearts of Oak*, JG was at his desk in Stanmore.

As the Suez landings did not take place until four months after my father's hasty return to London, I've sometimes wondered if that return was entirely necessary. While I was proud that he was involved in matters of national importance, I was also hurt that he missed what was an important milestone for me. The hurt was compounded by the fact that he never expressed any regret about it. It would have been so easy for him to drop me a note to say how sorry he was to have missed my passing-out parade and to congratulate me on passing my exams. But he did not. This placed another brick in the wall between us, and planted in me the seeds of a rebellion against all that he stood for, to the extent that for many years after his death I used to claim, not entirely lightheartedly, that if ever I had a difficult decision to take I would wonder what my father would do in similar circumstances, and do the opposite.

When the troops landed at Suez, the stock market plummeted. Believing the outbreak of World War III to be imminent, my father lost his nerve and sold out all his share holdings at rock bottom, halving the value of his modest estate overnight. I learnt from that.

19

I spent the following term at sea aboard the training ship HMS *Carron*, an old World War II destroyer. We slept in hammocks, thirty to a mess deck. We kept day and night watches, scrubbed decks, cleaned paintwork, polished brass, and peeled potatoes. I took turns in the wheelhouse, manned the sea boat, practiced coastal navigation, operated the ship's sonar, manned the four-point-five inch gun, and threw up into a bucket when the sea was rough.

In company with the other two ships of the training squadron, we crossed the Bay of Biscay and called in at the port of Leixões in Portugal, where I attended a cocktail party in a Portuguese fort and chatted with a very charming lady, who later became my mother in law. It was while visiting Leixões that I saw the sardine fishing fleet putting to sea and witnessed the poverty of the slum-dwellers who worked in the canning factory, where disease, child prostitution, and hunger were commonplace. This was to be the inspiration for my first novel, *The River Running By*.

From Portugal, we steamed on down to Gibraltar, where we drank Malaga at four pence a glass in the Trocadero and witnessed British matelots fighting in the streets and returning on board drunk. My eyes were opened, for the first time, to the fact that British sailors were not as pure minded, courteous, or healthy, as my mother had led me to believe.

Churchill was right: the Royal Navy ran on "rum, bum, and baccy." Sex, foul language, and soft pornography were closely woven into every aspect of life at sea in a destroyer. A box of free-issue condoms was kept on the gangway for liberty men. At any one time, the sick bay queue included half a dozen of the ship's company who had contracted venereal disease. The mess decks were decorated with full-frontal pin-ups, which, for some obscure reason, were permitted by the first lieutenant provided no pubic hair was on display. At sea during the night watches, we huddled against the funnel for warmth, snacking on potatoes that had been baked in the asbestos lagging in the boiler room, and passing round pornographic literature. While on watch in the wheelhouse, I was obliged to listen to the quartermaster and bosun's mate discussing the sexual orientation of other members of the ship's company; and a selection of pornographic gramophone records, some of which had strong overtones of pedophilia, did the rounds of the mess decks.

The ideal naval man, we were given to understand, was one who "worked hard and played hard"—who drank, smoked, and had sex wherever and whenever the opportunity arose. It was all part of the process of dehumanization. You can't train decent young people to commit the atrocities of war by inculcating decent habits and ideals. As the song goes in *South Pacific*, they have to be carefully taught.

We returned to Dartmouth as midshipmen the following term, and embarked on professional training designed to fit us for service in the Fleet. We attended lectures on gunnery, anti-submarine warfare, communications, cryptography, solar and astral navigation, radar, and nuclear, biological, and chemical warfare. In the classroom, we studied transmission systems, electric motors, calculus, and trigonometry.

Down at the engineering workshops at Sandquay we were introduced, after a security briefing, to nuclear physics. We were shown confidential films of the nuclear bomb bursts at Hiroshima and Nagasaki, and the tests at Bikini. Though I found the images of devastation shocking and felt that there was something intrinsically wrong about manufacturing such weapons, I had by this time been brainwashed into acceptance of whatever I was taught or trained to do. It took me many years to undo that process, and to purge myself of giving even tacit approval to the manufacture or possession of nuclear weapons.

No one talked much about the ethics of the nuclear deterrent, though one of the brightest of my term, Jeremy Boutwood, surprised us all by leaving the Navy at the end of his midshipman's time on the grounds of conscientious objection. I admired him for his moral courage, and admire him still. I believe nuclear weapons are the resort of cowardly nations, and that Britain's possession of them has played a major part not only in hastening our national decline, but also in motivating hatred and terrorism.

As midshipmen, we were given much more freedom, and were allowed to keep cars and motorbikes at the college. I bought, for £6, a James 98 cc motorbike, upon which I pottered up and down the steep Devon hills, going to see Audrey Hepburn in *Funny Face* three weeks running, and sipping sweet cider in the saloon bars of country pubs.

I was, in those days, a sanctimonious prig. Late one evening in Dartmouth, I walked past a small terraced cottage and overheard a monumental row going on inside, husband and wife yelling and shrieking at each other at the top of their voices. I stopped and listened and, during a lull, called in through the open window in my best Archangel Gabriel voice, "Have a little tolerance!" before striding quickly away. Another cause of shame happened late one night on a bus back from Paignton, when a woman passenger started drunkenly abusing all and sundry at the top of her voice. I glanced back and recognized her. It was Molly Prettyjohn. While the bus bumped along she crooned, sang, cursed, and cackled, to the annoyance and embarrassment of my fellow passengers. And again, I did something that I have since regretted. When I arrived at my stop, I paused before alighting and said, "You want to watch it, Molly. There are people around who know who you are."

I still hate myself for saying that. If only I had had the maturity and moral courage to sit with her and show her some of the human affection she so desperately needed. People don't become kleptomaniacs or go into drugs or prostitution because they are evil; they do so because they are in desperate need of love.

20

With some of his mother's legacy, my father bought an old converted fishing cutter, and one summer leave we went sailing together in the Solent. Built of pitch pine on oak before the Great War, *Fair Judgment* was an old-timer: forty-five feet overall, gaff rigged, with a nine-foot bowsprit, black hull, counter stern, and russet sails.

For a few happy days, we sailed about the Solent visiting my father's old haunts of Bembridge, Cowes, and Yarmouth. As a member of the Royal Engineers Yacht Club, he was entitled to wear the REYC yachting cap badge and to fly a defaced Blue Ensign. He had a sailing smock that had never been washed and was hardened with salt. It only took one afternoon in the sun to restore his tan, and I saw him unshaven for the first time in my life.

He took me out for pub lunches and suppers. Wherever we went, he fell quickly and easily into conversation with people. Set free from my mother and sisters, he was a changed man. I had never seen him so at ease with the world as I did during that short week we spent sailing together. I almost got to know him.

One afternoon while sailing up Southampton Water, we passed close to a Norwegian cruise liner. Instantly, my father became extremely animated. He stood up, waved his arms above his head, and sang the anthem of the Norwegian Resistance at the top of his voice.

Fifty years later, I found what might explain his affection for Norway and the Norwegians in a letter he wrote from Oslo to my mother in 1945, when he was engaged in restoring local government in outlying towns and villages. In the letter, he describes the disembarkation of King Haakon on his return from wartime exile in Britain, and the welcome in front of the city hall:

> Standing next to me was the daughter-in-law of Berg, the President of the High Court of Justice, who commanded and organized the Norwegian underground without ever being suspected by Jerry. She gave a sort of running commentary for us, and pointed out all the interesting personalities. At lunch time we had numerous drinks (captured champagne and cognac) and after that I had a snooze. In the evening we went to a dance given by a Scottish unit, which was a mixture of Holly-

> wood and the Highlands. The girls here are just battalions of Greta Garbo's, and they still have the most marvellous clothes. Quite put the poor Parisiennes in the shade with their turnout, but where it all comes from is a mystery. There's nothing in the shops, and if you are a kid with good sound clothes and shoes, you may be sure they were a present from Sweden.

In the same letter, he announced his decision to extend his service after the war:

> I am so glad that you agree that that is best, darling. It would be a misery to drop down to what is almost penury, instead of putting a little by, and giving the kids their chance. Also, I feel that if Labour <u>does</u> get in, they will make such a hash of it that they will be thrown out at the next election, and then perhaps we could make a come back. It's quite likely that a civvy job might grow out of it, as you say. Also, we could probably arrange it so that you could come out to me between leaves, and have a little married life together!

I was now in my nineteenth year and had seen enough of naval life to recognize that naval values were incompatible with those of the Brethren. This didn't worry me overmuch, but I did feel a need to face up to the fact that continuing any sort of pretence to my parents that I was obedient to the precepts and doctrines of the Brethren was hypocritical. So I wrote to my father and put it to him bluntly that I felt unable to continue the pretence any further, asking him what he thought of my applying to the Church of England for baptism and admission to communion. He typed a three-page letter in reply.

> My dear Charles,
>
> Many thanks for your letter. You set out your problem so clearly that it puts me on the spot. Christian life for an officer is more than a problem, of course; it's a perpetual struggle. I'm afraid I've been worsted in that struggle many times, but you can take solid comfort from that part of my experience, which has shown that the patience and ingenuity of God are inexhaustible and beyond comprehension, even in retrospect. If it had not been for this, I should long ago have become a castaway [...] I don't think that your smoking or taking a drink in social intercourse has anything to do with the breth-

ren there. You have never asked to be received into the fellowship of the Assembly, and you have not in any way subjected your conscience to what they may or may not think fitting. Even so, there are several brethren in the Assembly who are neither teetotalers nor non-smokers, and in the face of Col. 2. 20-23, I don't see how any veto could be imposed. That passage, together with Romans 14 and 1. Cor. 10. 19-33 are very much to the point.

My position was very different. I was baptized at 17 and received into fellowship at Cholmeley Hall. Mother was then a strict teetotaler, and I couldn't smoke in the house. I started smoking at 18, when I went to Sandhurst, but the ban on smoking at home wasn't lifted until a Crusader leader, Jack Freegard, was on leave from France, and asked if he could smoke when he came to tea.

I was very bitter about that time, first over not getting into the Navy, and then, just after I was commissioned in 1918, because I was crossed in love. I had nursed a romantic passion for Francis Harris from the moment I first saw her in 1915, when we moved to Muswell Hill from Enfield after my father's death. Between then and 1918, I had never walked a hundred yards alone with her, seen her with her hat off, or had anything that could be called a connected conversation with her! It was very hard in those days.

I had neither the art nor the will to disguise my passion, so Frances must have known of it. After being commissioned in 1918 I came home on leave, and somehow persuaded my mother to get Frances to come up to London with us—I think to buy some hymn books! It sounds ridiculous today, but I regarded this occasion as promoting our acquaintance to the point where I could write to her. It was quite an outpouring, and in the letter, I asked her what she thought about smoking. She wrote a sweet little note back to say that she had become engaged to be married to […], and a rotten husband he was to her. […]

Article XXVI of the C. of E. Articles of Religion declares that the unworthiness of Ministers hinders not the effect of the sacrament […] it is nevertheless important to be assured that the person from whom you receive baptism is not only a true believer but a faithful minister of the gospel. If you were fully persuaded that it would be right to seek communion of that Church, I think it would be of great value to talk it over with someone about whom there is no doubt in that respect—say,

Maurice Wood or Mr. Turvey at North Finchley. I am sure you will find that the people in the denominations at large with whom you can have any real communion are few, and there is as much difference between Maurice Wood and the mere professor as there is between the professor and any of the brethren you may have met.

Of course you know that I am not really detached about these things, and I am firmly convinced that the worship God seeks cannot be reduced to forms of service, though the worship of the heart may transcend the form. Don't do anything in a rush, and regard this juncture in your experience as a proof that God our Father has a way for you to follow, which he can show

Must stop here, or the post will go.

I read his letter with impatience and dismay. Its musty language and exclusivity reflected attitudes that were now light years from those that my time in the Royal Navy had inculcated, and it came as a shock to realize how far I had moved away from the pettifogging doctrines of the Brethren. There was little warmth in those neatly typed lines, and I despaired at his references to Biblical texts. I had given him a rare opportunity to give me his open-handed, positive, and loving support—to say, in effect, "Yes! Go for it!"

But he blew it.

My new Divisional Officer was Lieutenant Commander Bertie Tower, an urbane, imperturbable gentleman who did not look at all like a naval officer. He wore pebble glasses and had a bad stoop. His father, Vice Admiral Sir Thomas Tower, had served on Churchill's war staff, and his brother Philip had been decorated for gallantry.

One Easter leave he took four of us midshipman sailing in the Drake Division yacht *Martlet*. The college yachts had no engines, but we navigated safely across the English Channel in a force six gale to St. Malo, where I met Jacqueline, the sexy daughter of the local baker. She taught me, among other things, how to kiss, and gave me a little silver skull with emerald eyes as a memento. I went on another cruise to St. Malo with Bertie in the summer leave. One sunny afternoon when we were tied up alongside in the inner harbor, three girls came by, and I asked them aboard. They were nurses from Bristol and I fell in love with the one with mousey hair and glasses. Her name was Vivienne, and on our last evening together, while sitting on the harbor wall looking at the sunset, she told me that one day I would make someone a wonderful husband. I hadn't thought about being anyone's husband until then, but her remark gave me ideas.

I spent the following term at sea in the frigate HMS *Roebuck* and exchanged letters with Vivienne regularly each month. I invited her to the Dartmouth Christmas Ball of 1957, but she was unable to accept, so I agreed to take the friend of a friend instead. My blind date—and, as it turned out, wife-to-be—was one of three trainee nursery nurses from St. Thomas' Babies' Hostel in the southeast of London. She seemed very mature and self-confident, and I felt nervous of her. I knew already that she was a Roman Catholic, and this added a certain mystery and attraction. That evening at the ball, we took off together for a walk in the dark on the playing fields, and by the time we returned to the ball, I knew that she was the one.

There was an Irish song popular at the time about a milkmaid who declares, "I will and I must get married, for the humor is on me now." That was how I felt: I told myself that if I tried hard enough, I could believe anything I chose, and that the requirement of my becoming a Catholic need not be a major obstacle. So, one evening in my last term at Dartmouth, I knocked on the RC Chaplain's door and told him I wanted to convert. He gave me a booklet entitled *What Catholics Believe*, which I read from cover to cover that evening.

I didn't need much convincing. I was at an age when one thinks of sex almost constantly, and I found the prospect of praying to the Virgin Mary, making the sign of the Cross, and being forbidden to use contraception particularly sexy. Confession was an added bonus. I looked forward to being able to off-load all and every kind of sexual guilt through a grille to an anonymous priest. Also, I had a deep-seated need to jump as far away as possible from the dreary nay-saying Brethren into a religion where, as Hilaire Belloc put it, "there's always laughter and good red wine."

Having marched past in our sub lieutenants' uniforms, we finally shook the dust of Dartmouth from our feet, and gathered in London at the Dorchester Hotel to dine and dance with our girl friends and wives-to-be.

Five days later, I joined my first ship.

21

We had been required to state our preferences for where in the world we would like to serve: in the Far East, the Mediterranean, the Persian Gulf, the Home Fleet, or the West Indies. Wishing to stay close to the object of my passion, I chose the Home Fleet, and was appointed to a coastal minesweeper in the Fishery Protection Squadron.

I joined HMS *Wasperton* at Chatham Dockyard on the ship's commissioning day. On my arrival, having listened to my breathless, "Sub Lieutenant Wheeler come aboard to join, sir," the first lieutenant, a debutante's delight called Barry, told me to go to his cabin and remain there until the commissioning ceremony was over. It wasn't the best way to start my time on board. Sitting in Barry's cabin, listening to the band playing and the shouted orders on the quayside, I reflected that I had been excluded all over again.

The captain of HMS *Wasperton* was a jolly, ginger haired Welsh lieutenant commander with a beaky nose who claimed, with good reason if looks are anything to go by, to be a descendant of Lloyd George. He had been promoted from the lower deck and had three rows of war medals. He drank fifteen bottles of Gordon's gin a month, five bottles of Vat 69 whisky, a couple of Sackville amontillado sherry, a bottle of five-star VSOP brandy, and a bottle of Drambuie. I know, because I was the wardroom wine and spirits caterer.

Barry, a suede shoes and after-shave man, tried valiantly to keep up with him, and within a few months developed a rather puffy complexion as a result. I shared a cabin with Barry for a while, but was driven out by the stench of his socks and sought refuge in the cramped quarters of the chartroom under the bridge, with the light of the 974 radar beam sweeping round and round at my feet, and the Decca navigator hiccupping intermittently over my head.

The navigator, John, was a small, dapper little man whose father had been an aide-de-camp to the late King George VI. John was deeply cynical about authority and had a knack of opening his mouth and putting his foot in it. He and I went on an outing to Stirling castle one afternoon, and I was foolish enough to try to counsel him into adopting a less sarcastic attitude, to which he took deep offence. He left the ship under a cloud after a few months and committed suicide a year or so after that.

The correspondence officer, Brian Watling, was an urbane, meticulous, and rather churchy sub lieutenant doing national service. He had a First in law from Cambridge and drove a red Jaguar to impress his clients. He trained for the bar under Sir Christmas Humphreys and acted as best man at my wedding. Later, he became a QC, served as assistant to the Director of Public Prosecutions, and took silk as a high court judge.

I was given an assortment of jobs in the ship, for which my training at Dartmouth had provided little preparation. At the age of nineteen, I was the gunnery officer, the explosives accounting officer, the divisional officer to the engineering and electrical ratings and—the most important and time-consuming of all—the wardroom wine caterer.

At the beginning of the commission, the wardroom steward and I tried to conform to proper service procedure and run a bar chit system. An officer would write out a chit for a G&T (gin and tonic) or HN (horse's neck), sign it, and put it in a box, and the following morning Steward Jannaway would enter the amounts in the Wardroom Wine and Spirit Book.

Gin cost two pence a slug; whisky was four pence, and Drambuie a shilling. The captain was an inveterate entertainer of equally hard-drinking captains from other minesweepers. On arrival in port, he used to order the hoisting of the "gin pennant" at the yardarm to signal that he requested the pleasure of the company of other commanding officers on board for drinks. The sheer volume of booze consumed at these gatherings made accounting by the chit system impossible, and Barry decided that we should give up writing chits and use a slate instead. But late at night with much liquor inside them, the captain and his guests were more inclined to draw diagrams of minesweeping maneuvers on the slate than to enter the fifth double gin or the third tot of Vat 69, so I resorted to the simpler and quicker system of mustering the wines and spirits at the beginning and end of the month, finding out how much had been consumed, and fudging the daily entries in the columns of the Wine and Spirit Book.

We boozed our way round the British Isles, trying to catch French crabbers fishing inside the three-mile limit, or German trawlers using nets with illegally small gauges; and when we sailed round the Shetland Isles, we saw the vast Russian fishing fleet, with attendant factory ships and intelligence-gathering trawlers.

We came nearest to success in our fishery protection duties when we arrested a French crabber close inshore off Lundy Island. We took the skipper to court, but Mr. Harman, the owner of Lundy, spoke in his defense, arguing that the waters around Lundy were his, and that he had given this particular crabber permission to fish inshore. We lost the case.

At each new port we visited we threw a cocktail party for the local dignitaries, at which the captain homed unerringly in on the most willing—or deemed likely-to-be-willing—women. One of his late-night ploys was to say to a lady guest, "My dear, I do believe that you might be a perfect woman." He would then produce a measuring tape and explain that the perfect woman was one whose nipples and neck formed an equilateral triangle with sides six inches long. The lady guest was persuaded, in the interests of science, to undergo measurement, which was only possible when her top garments had been removed and her bra straps released to ensure that her breasts were not, as our captain put it, "bowzed in."

John's replacement, Basil, wasn't interested in birds, booze or bonking; but Mike, Brian's replacement, was, and we took to phoning up the local hospital in advance of a port visit to provide (or "lay on" as we termed it) a couple of willing nurses for mutual entertainment and temporary friendship. One of these, a trainee physiotherapist at Poole General Hospital, knitted me a very nice navy blue woolen hat with a yellow pom-pom on top. Thank you, Gillian.

In those far-off days before we sunk the Argentine cruiser *Belgrano* or sent submarines to sea with nuclear missiles capable of burning a few million civilians to a cinder with a single salvo, the Navy was still highly thought of, and young naval officers were in demand wherever one of HM ships put into port. On the Isle of Man, I was entertained by an Anglican bishop who fondled my knee and invited me to stay the night in his palace. I declined, but inevitably had to suffer the adolescent wit of my fellow officers about kissing his ring. At Fleetwood, I gave a talk to the local comprehensive school about Nelson and the Battle of Trafalgar, the memory of which still causes an inward squirm; and it was also at Fleetwood that a wealthy trawler skipper gave me five pounds to take his daughter on an outing to Blackpool. We traveled on the top of a double-decker bus, each acutely aware of the yawning social gulf between us, and saw Elizabeth Taylor in *Cat on a Hot Tin Roof*. By unspoken mutual agreement, there was no snog.

I was the only officer on board over Christmas, 1958. The ship was sitting in a dockyard basin in Rosyth, undergoing maintenance. We were "out of routine," which meant that we were not obliged to conform to normal naval ceremonial. A few days before Christmas, a signal came from Flag Officer Scotland, the local admiral, ordering ships to dress over all on Christmas Day. Being out of routine we were not obliged to do this, but I thought it might cheer everyone up, and told Leading Seaman Garrett, who was fifteen years my senior and had seen much war service, that I intended that the ship would be dressed overall.

My directive brought the ship's company to the brink of mutiny. Garrett buttonholed me and asked if he could speak "man to man," a request to which I foolishly agreed. He told me that he wasn't going to take orders from a jumped up midshipman, and that the ship would not, repeat not, be dressed over all.

This, being blatant disobedience, sent my pulse into overdrive. But I was on my own, and knew that I would have to deal with it on my own. I also knew that if I gave in to him, my authority would be worth nothing in the ship.

I opened the safe in the ship's office and took out a confidential book called *Mutiny in the Royal Navy*, which I read all the way through. It detailed mutinies dating back to 1919, including the mutiny at Newport in which Captain Kennedy, father of the journalist Ludovic Kennedy, had been involved, and which had cost him—quite unjustly—his career. It also contained a detailed account of the mutiny at Invergordon in 1931, when the men of the Atlantic Fleet went on strike over an inequitable pay cut.

Having thus briefed myself, I sent for Garrett and told him that, although I was prepared to concede that I was wrong to order the ship to be dressed overall when we were out of routine, we were now on the brink of something that could be catastrophic for him, particularly as he was at the end of his time in the Navy, and that the only way to avoid that catastrophe was for my legitimate order to be carried out.

He saw the sense of this, and the ship was duly dressed with signal flags from bow to stern on Christmas Day; but on Boxing Day when I mustered the hands, someone had scrawled WHEELER MUST GO on the bulkhead. I had it cleaned off immediately, and was glad when the other officers came back off leave and I could take two weeks off to go skiing in the Cairngorms.

The incident sparked my interest in mutiny and its causes, and was in part the inspiration for my novel *Jannaway's Mutiny*, and its sequel *The Raging of the Sea*.

Towards the end of my time on board HMS *Wasperton*, the ship visited Florø on the west coast of Norway. I had, by this time, taken over as the ship's navigator, and the captain directed me to plan a passage that would take us on a tour of the fjords before arrival.

I stood the morning watch. We arrived off the coast before dawn on a clear but bitterly cold morning. At a modest eight knots, we threaded our way between the islands, sometimes passing through narrows only fifty yards wide, with rocks and mountains rising up on either side. There were only three of us on the open bridge: the captain, the signalman, and myself, and we all found the experience of steering our little ship between those silent islands calming and uplifting.

In this mood of spiritual elation, we arrived at Florø. Our visit was the first to that port by a British warship since before the beginning of the war, and we had been assured of a warm reception. But there was no reception. A solitary fisherman in yellow sea boots took our lines. I had got the time zone wrong. We were an hour late.

There were a number of close shaves aboard HMS *Wasperton*, including a collision with a jetty, the theft of a bicycle, going aground in the Isles of Scilly, and the Captain's accidental reversing of a Morris 8 saloon onto the ship's forecastle. But I was the nearest anyone came to a court martial aboard that dodgy little sweeper. As the ship's tobacco caterer it was my unofficial duty to juggle the figures to make the stock musters agree with the quarterly returns to the Customs & Excise. Every month, six tobacco coupons, each coupon good for the purchase of one hundred cigarettes, were issued to every member of the ship's company that had signed a declaration to the effect that he used tobacco, pressure being applied to non-smokers to sign the declaration so that their tobacco coupons could be used to buy extra cigarettes for the wardroom. At the end of each month, I had to destroy unused coupons in the presence of a witness and return a certificate to that effect to the Customs, countersigned by the captain.

It all went wrong one month when I destroyed a whole sheet of tobacco coupons in error, with the result that the number of cigarettes actually sold was vastly in excess of the number of coupons available to support the monthly return. This was a serious matter. The Navy's duty-free privileges were jealously guarded, and cases of embezzlement were court martial offences.

I went along to the captain's cabin and told him what had happened. "Well, Sub," he said. "You'll just have to fix it, won't you?"

So I did, and felt proud of the ingenuity of my method, which was to make, for three months in succession, one return to the naval base supply officer at Port Edgar, and a different one to the Customs and Excise officer at Leith, each of which the captain obligingly countersigned.

The only way we could have been found out was if the two had compared accounts. This did not happen. I got away with it—and that, I was beginning to learn, was all that really mattered in the Royal Navy.

22

In the summer of 1958, I spent my two weeks' leave visiting wife-to-be in Portugal. I stayed with her family at Leça da Palmeira, a few miles north of Porto. Their lifestyle was colonial. We changed for dinner, and I was introduced by my father-in-law-to-be to the subtleties of Mackenzie's white port on the rocks before lunch and the nutty flavor of a good tawny after dinner.

It was August, and the time of the annual pilgrimage to Fatima, which I attended. I witnessed the candlelit procession in which an image of the Virgin Mary was carried up to the basilica, while thousands of pilgrims and penitents recited decades of the Holy Rosary and sang mournful hymns to Our Lady. I had misgivings about such idolatry, but suppressed them. After all, I was in love, and love has a habit of transcending theological skepticism.

After the procession, I spent an uncomfortable night in a seminary dormitory in the company of some very devout young Catholic men from Oxford. This was a far cry indeed from HMS *Wasperton*'s wardroom, the captain's search for a perfect woman, creative accounting, and the stench of the first lieutenant's sea boot stockings.

The following morning, after my Oxford companions had been to Confession, we attended high mass, though as an un-baptized outsider, I could not take communion. So I sat alone while wife-to-be, her brother and his Oxford friends went up to take the wafer to the whispered *corpus domini nostri Jesu Christi custodiat animam tuam in vitam aeternam* of a Jesuit priest. Watching from a row of empty seats as my wife-to-be, wearing a black mantilla, knelt to accept the wafer, I was suddenly back at Oakleigh Hall, sitting straight backed and open-eyed as my father, mother, and sisters took communion, and the bread and wine passed me by.

When we had bought our hand carved images of the Blessed Virgin at the stalls outside the basilica (I didn't overturn any tables, but the thought did cross my mind) and were speeding northward over the cobbles to Porto, I knew that what I wanted above all was to *belong*, and then and there made up my mind to go ahead and convert to Catholicism.

The thought of finally breaking free from the Brethren and starting a new life as a member of the Catholic Church with all its tradition and authority behind me was spiritually invigorating. The smells, bells, candles, and Ave Maria's had not been in vain. Fatima had done the trick.

HMS *Wasperton* was based at Port Edgar, ten miles from Edinburgh, under the Forth rail bridge. Soon after returning off leave, I introduced myself to Father O'Hanlon, the local priest, who, over cups of weak tea and digestive biscuits, expounded an impressive array of Catholic doctrines: the difference between mortal and venal sin, the Immaculate Conception, the Real Presence of the Body of Christ, Papal Infallibility, the Assumption of Our Lady, Limbo, the Sacraments as outward signs of inward grace, Confession, Communion, Ordination, Holy Matrimony, Extreme Unction—and the mortal sin of "spilling the seed" by whatever means, whether by contraception, *coitus interruptus*, or masturbation. It certainly came as a quite shock to learn that every time I masturbated, my soul died; and I sensed that there was some sort of contradiction lurking in the fact that having a wet dream, however enjoyable, was not considered sinful by the Church.

All the same, I threw myself into this theological game of snakes and ladders with zeal. I relished the smell of incense and the tinkle of bells at the Consecration when the priest changed a packet of wafers into the body and blood of Christ. I liked the bustle of the RC cathedral in Edinburgh, where people knelt at chairs turned back to front, where I could smell the pungent body odors of people queuing for Confession, overhear the whisperings in the confessional, see the glowing piety in the teary eyes of an old man emerging from that dark box, and, when I had bought yet another Catholic Truth Society pamphlet to add to my collection, touch the salt-laden holy water to my forehead as I made the sign of the Cross and emerged into the worldly bustle of Edinburgh.

I was not so much embracing the Catholic Faith as enacting it. In my heart of hearts I knew that I was, effectively, "playing at being" a Catholic. But driving me on was the knowledge that if I wanted to marry wife-to-be (which I did) I would have to maintain the pretence and go through with conversion, piously quoting to myself Christ's admonition, "Be ye not unequally yoked together" as authority.

Besides, I was still laboring under the delusion that provided I tried hard enough I could make myself believe anything I liked—never dreaming for one moment that I would meet with any great opposition from my parents.

But on that score, I was in for a surprise.

My family name, Gidley, had special significance for my father. It comes from a hamlet perched on the edge of Dartmoor in Devon called Gidleigh. The name is derived from Gydda's (or Githa's) Lea. Gydda was the wife of Godwyn, Earl of Wessex, and was the mother of Harold II, killed at the Battle of Hastings in 1066.

After the battle, when Gydda had pleaded in vain with William the Conqueror to be given the body of her son for Christian burial, she fled west to Exeter, where she tried to rally the men of Devon for a counter-strike against the invading Normans. But her little army was vastly outnumbered, and she fled to "Gydda's Lea" on the edge of Dartmoor.

On the arrival of the Norman army, Gydda escaped by an underground tunnel and made her way to the north coast of Devon, from where she took ship to the island of Flatholm in the Severn Estuary; and from there she sailed with her retinue to the Low Countries, where she remained until her death.

My father took pride in our link with the last Saxon King of England. The Gidley family is neither famous nor notorious: doctors, lawyers, and civic dignitaries are much in evidence in the family tree, and the name Gidley will be found in a stained glass window in Exeter town hall. A Mr. Chidley sailed as a gentleman adventurer aboard the flagship Ark Royal to do battle with the Spanish Armada in 1588; a Bartholomew Gidley was knighted for his services to King Charles I, and William of Orange was godfather to another Gidley when he landed at Brixham in 1689 to take the throne of England.

There was, therefore, a very strong anti-Catholic tradition in our family, so when I broke the news to my parents that I was taking instruction with a view to conversion, a Catholic cat was put fairly among Protestant pigeons.

Hoping to reassure my parents, I paid a flying visit to 67 Brent Way one evening when my ship was at Chatham. Perhaps things might have been different had my parents told me how desperately worried they were—or, better still, that whatever decision I took they would still love and support me. But hatred of Roman Catholicism outweighed parental love, and I found myself being treated almost as a pariah.

I have forgotten much of what was said, but I do remember that my father stayed out of the room for most of the time, probably too upset or angry to speak to me. The argument between us boiled down to the interpretation of what Christ meant when he said to Peter, "Upon this rock I will build my church." The whole question of Papal authority and infallibility hinged on these words, Protestants believing that the "rock" referred to was Peter's words, "Thou art the Christ, the son of the living God," and Catholics believing that the rock was

Peter himself, to whom Jesus gave the power to absolve sin, and promised that whatever Peter might bind or loose on earth would be bound or loosed in heaven. It is that single text which forms the basis for the Roman Catholic Church's immense authority, for if you argue the toss with the Pope, you are, according to this doctrine, arguing the toss with God's representative on Earth.

While my family argued that Christians reading the Scriptures were guided by the Holy Spirit into all truth, I advocated the Catholic line that, because of the unbroken verbal tradition from St. Peter to the current incumbent at the Vatican, the Catholic Church had a unique and infallible authority, vested in it by God in the person of Jesus Christ.

However hard Protestants and Catholics may try to play it down, this question still lies at the heart of the disagreement between them and, I suggest, has been responsible down the centuries for wrecking the lives and happiness of countless men, women, and children.

In the event, my brief visit achieved nothing. When I returned to Chatham late that evening and went aboard HMS *Wasperton*, I knew that as far as religion was concerned, there was no hope of reconciliation between us.

Soon after my twenty-first birthday, I walked up the hill to the Church of Our Lady at Port Edgar and, in the presence of one witness, was baptized into the Roman Catholic Church. A few weeks later, I received a letter from my father in which he told me that, while he could in the future welcome me under his roof as he would an acquaintance or friend, he would no longer be able to do so as his brother in Christ. And, using a piece of emotional blackmail that hurt me to the quick, he warned that my conversion to Catholicism might well kill my mother.

I read his letter once through, then tore it up in disgust. There didn't seem any point of contact left between us.

23

After leaving HMS *Wasperton*, I was appointed to HMS *Saintes*, an open bridge destroyer of World War II vintage. The ship was commissioned in March 1960 at Devonport, and I took wife-to-be along to the ceremony. I discovered that I was the senior Catholic on board, and as such had to recite Hail Mary's on the Bofors gun deck while the majority of the ship's company sang "O God our Help in Ages Past" on the jetty. Once again, I found myself to be a member of a religious minority.

HMS *Saintes* was not the happiest of ships. During our commission, the captain sacked the first lieutenant, the explosives accounting officer was invalided out of the ship with ulcers, the supply officer was hospitalized with an infection, the engineer officer was brought to the brink of a nervous breakdown, the navigator threatened to resign his commission, and I became run-down and was confined to my bunk for two weeks with gastric influenza and boils in my ears.

Our captain was a dour man, promoted to commander too early for his own good. He employed a series of catch phrases with which to taunt his officers. "Not good enough, not good enough at all!" he would say, or, on his arrival on the bridge, "What's going on? What's going on?" Then there were his eternal, "Naught out of ten!" "Sharpen up, officer-of-the-watch!" "You miserable officer!" "Do better!" or, more personally, "Put a bomb under Wheeler!"

As correspondence officer, I had to present the daily correspondence to the captain for his perusal, type—immaculately—the multitude of his letters for signature, and ensure that the weekly, monthly, and quarterly returns were made on time to a variety of senior authorities. It was also my job to collect armfuls of "weekly books" for the captain's signature, write out railway warrants, type out punishment warrants, and attend Requestmen and Defaulters, with all the relevant papers and service documents at the ready. This meant that I spent a great deal of time standing at the captain's elbow, which gave him ample opportunity to hound me to his heart's content.

HMS *Saintes* was chosen to act as escort destroyer to the Royal Yacht, with the Queen and Duke of Edinburgh embarked, on a cruise down the west coast of Africa. We had a new first lieutenant now, Keith. He had recently been on loan to the Royal Australian Navy, and brought a breath of fresh Aussie air with him.

His brisk good humor and positive leadership counteracted the malevolence of our perfectionist captain, and boosted the ship's company morale.

Following in *Britannia*'s wake, we sailed southward into the tropics, visiting Bathurst, Monrovia, Freetown, and Takoradi. As the sun rose higher and we approached the equator, the men off watch took to sunbathing naked on the upper deck. The captain didn't like this, but the first lieutenant permitted it, so that when we were out of binocular sight of the royal yacht, the decks were littered with naked sailors doing what they called "bronzy-bronzy." This must have put ideas into young heads, because one night two teenage junior seamen were caught indulging in oral sex. They were placed under close arrest, brought before the captain on charges of gross indecency, sentenced by warrant to ninety days' punishment at the Royal Naval Detention Quarters, and dismissed the Service.

After six months in home waters, we sailed in company with the First Destroyer Squadron to join the Mediterranean Fleet. Malta, where we were based, was not the best possible advertisement for Catholicism. I was disturbed to discover that priests supplemented their income by demanding exorbitantly high payments of penance from the poor, and that a man's livelihood could be jeopardized by irregular attendance at Mass. I tried to convince myself that English Catholicism was different from the Maltese variety, but couldn't help reflecting that if there were varieties of Catholicism scattered about the world, the Church could not claim to be catholic in the true sense. There were other aspects of Catholicism that troubled me. I didn't like the gory images of Christ on the Cross, the sad-faced Madonna's, the indulgences, the repetitious litanies—and particularly that self-effacing prayer to the Virgin Mary that went: "To thee to we send up our sighs, mourning and weeping in this veil of tears."

I was already in a state of growing disaffection. But my colors were nailed to the mast and there was no going back. So, in spite of misgivings, I contacted the shore based RC chaplain, and told him that I wanted to be confirmed. This ceremony was performed in private by the Bishop of Malta, whose ring I was obliged to kiss.

My wife-to-be came out to Malta in the spring of 1961, and we became engaged to be married. A few months later Iraq threatened to invade Kuwait, and HMS *Saintes* was ordered to sail at short notice for duties in the Persian Gulf. For a month, we trailed around at high speed over the glassy waters of the Persian Gulf, keeping station on the aircraft carrier HMS *Victorious* while her jets practiced the technique of over-the-shoulder toss bombing used for the delivery of the nuclear weapons secretly carried by all British aircraft carriers at that time. It was

August. There was no air conditioning in the ship, and the temperature and humidity between decks became intolerable. The wardroom was full of cockroaches and the ship's ventilation system was inadequate. Along with many of the ship's company, I took to sleeping on the upper deck under the stars.

The Kuwait crisis over, we returned to the Mediterranean, where we again acted as escort to the Royal Yacht, this time in the Greek Islands. The ship was allowed a break of a few days, during which we anchored in a bay off Skyros, put a boat ashore and renovated "a corner of a foreign field that is for ever England"—Rupert Brooke's grave, which stands in a peaceful olive grove where nightingales sing and goatherds tend their flocks.

I was due to leave the ship in March 1962, and my fiancée and I planned an April wedding. I was still only twenty-three and would not qualify for full marriage allowance. As my fiancée came from a wealthy family, I was concerned that my lieutenant's pay would not be enough to support her in the manner to which she was accustomed.

A solution to this problem offered itself one bitterly cold January evening when the ship was on anti-submarine exercises off Portland. The helicopter we were exercising with was breaking off to return to the naval air station at Yeovilton, and David Gunn, an amusing and debonair aviator who kept a pet skunk on board and entertained us, mainly in E Flat, on the wardroom piano, turned to me, pointed at the departing Wessex helicopter and said, "There you are, Gidley, he'll be having hot buttered toast in the mess in half an hour—and he's paid twenty-five bob a day extra for the privilege, the lucky bugger."

Having no wish to become a gunnery officer, communications officer, or torpedo and anti-submarine officer, and having had my application to serve in submarines blocked by our nay-saying captain, I typed out a formal letter applying to be considered as a volunteer for duties as a helicopter pilot in the Fleet Air Arm.

The captain forwarded my application without delay and I received a reply in quick time. The Fleet Air Arm was always on the lookout for aircrew, and was not above pressing some to enlist, so I was given a warm welcome and told that as soon I had passed my air medical I would start training as a helicopter pilot.

24

I was married at a nuptial high Mass in the Church of Our Lady of Ransome, in the seaside town of Eastbourne on the south coast of England. Unfortunately, the rift with my father remained, and he refused to enter the church to witness the ceremony. He and my mother attended the reception, but I don't remember speaking more than a few words to either of them. I didn't really feel that I belonged to their family any more.

After a five-day honeymoon, I joined the Royal Naval College at Greenwich to start a six-month course in staff work. Having been passed fit for aircrew duties, I telephoned the Admiralty to report the fact, only to be told that they had enough helicopter pilots for the time being and that I was to be trained as a fixed wing pilot instead. I made a quiet protest about this, so the following day a commander and a Royal Marine captain—both aviators—came down from the Ministry of Defence to the college to interview me. They advised me to accept that I would have to train as fixed wing aircrew. I pointed out that I had volunteered to fly helicopters, not fixed wing, and said that I did not want to fly fixed wing.

"What if I say no?" I asked.

There was a stunned silence; then the Royal Marine captain turned to the commander and said, "I don't think we heard that, did we?"

By then I knew enough about the Royal Navy to be aware that if I refused to specialize as a fixed wing pilot, my confidential papers would be marked L.M.F.—Lacking in Moral Fiber—and I could kiss goodbye any hopes of a successful or even interesting career.

After the interview, I walked up and down outside the college, staring across the River Thames and wondering what would become of me. Deaths in the Fleet Air Arm were commonplace at that time. Two of my term had already been killed in air accidents, and only a few weeks before, six aircrew of 849 Squadron had been killed when two Gannet aircraft had collided during a night exercise off Cornwall. All the same, I felt I had no option but to go ahead and train as a fixed-wing pilot. I did not have the self-confidence to raise two fingers to the Royal Navy, but at the same time doubted whether I would survive more than a few years.

I felt as if I was being swept along on a tide of events, and that my life was completely out of control.

Being press-ganged into becoming a fixed wing pilot turned out to be no bad thing, as I found that the "Airy Fairies" of the Fleet Air Arm were quite different in their outlook from the "Fish Heads" of the surface fleet. In the world of aviation, either you get back in one piece or you don't. All that counts is your flying ability. Rank is of little importance, and religion none whatsoever.

I started flying training in September 1962 at Linton-on-Ouse, a Royal Air Force base in the Vale of York. After six months on the Jet Provost, I graduated to the Vampire for advanced flying training. The Vampire was the aircraft that had overawed me at Lympne air show fifteen years before. It had been the RAF's front line fighter and was the successor to the Spitfire. Its performance was superior to that of the Jet Provost in every respect, though the cockpit layout was somewhat archaic. Take-off acceleration was much higher than the Jet Provost's, as was the climbing speed. Landing was more difficult too: you had to flare the aircraft in the last stages, keeping the nose high so that you lost sight of the runway. This was particularly challenging at night.

Within a month or so I was having difficulty and was in danger of failing the course. I was taken aside by my squadron commander, who warned me that if I, the course leader, had to be chopped, it would have a serious effect on the morale of my course.

I found instrument flying and night flying particularly difficult. I was living on my nerves. One night I returned home at two in the morning to the little bungalow we rented on the outskirts of York and, trying not to wake my wife, entered the bedroom in the dark and stubbed my bare toe on the sharp metal foot of the paraffin heater. "Clot!" my wife said from the warmth of her bed as I hopped about in agony, and the next I knew, my hands were at her throat. I would never have imagined that I could do such a thing; but nor had I imagined that learning to bring a Vampire jet to a safe landing at night could be so demanding in terms of nervous energy.

The summer weeks went by and our Final Handling Tests approached. One July afternoon I fell out of a high-level loop at 28,000 feet and entered an inadvertent spin that was so fast that the Vale of York was nothing but a blur below me. Training took over: I went through the recovery drill and, after a delay during which the rate of rotation at first increased, I pulled out of the dive having lost about fifteen thousand feet.

There was a Flight Safety poster in the students' crew room that read, "Blessed is he that expects the worst, for he shall not be disappointed." That came true one afternoon at Rufforth airfield when I had a tire burst while doing a formation take off. The aircraft left the runway, the undercarriage collapsed and after a belly slide of a few hundred yards, we came to rest with our nose five yards from a concrete bunker. We had a cigarette and cup of tea in the control tower, then I and my instructor got into another aircraft, did another couple of formation take-offs and landings, and returned to Linton for tea.

That accident proved to be a turning point for me. Aborted take-offs were renowned for their fatal consequences. The worst had happened, and I had not been disappointed.

I passed out with wings on my arm a few weeks later, after which my wife and I packed up our things and set out for our new home in Helston, three hundred miles away on the south coast of Cornwall.

I was twenty-five years old. I qualified for marriage allowance, a married quarter, and flying pay—and I was the proud father of a gorgeous three-month-old-daughter.

For the first time in my life, I considered myself well off.

25

JG was now sixty-four, and the prospect of retirement was not a rosy one. Having complete faith in Divine providence, he had made no provision for his retirement. He had no pension, no insurance and next to no capital. Other worries added to the strain. His only son had turned Catholic and was dicing with death as a Fleet Air Arm pilot at a time when relations between the Soviet Union and the West were at their worst and it seemed that we were on the brink of all-out nuclear war. Neither of his daughters was married or had any prospect of marrying—and only a year before, he had been forced to sell his beloved *Fair Judgment* after nearly foundering in a gale and being lifted off by a Royal Navy helicopter.

"Poor Daddy!" my mother used to say of him in later years. Poor Daddy indeed: nothing he had started had turned out well. Except for a few years when he was such a roaring success as a cavalry subaltern, his life had been a perpetual struggle against the slings and arrows of outrageous fortune.

As the date of his retirement grew nearer, he began dreaming of seeing out the rest of his days in a cottage by the sea. But my mother was not keen on the idea. She liked the stability of 67 Brent Way, the meeting at Cholmley Hall, and the Women's Missionary Fellowship once a week.

In the summer of 1963, they rented a thatched cottage in Hampshire's Meon Valley, where they had a brief taste of genteel luxury. It was the first vacation they had taken alone together since his return from the war fifteen years before.

That autumn, on our way from Yorkshire to Cornwall, I took my new family to stay for a weekend at 67 Brent Way, and JG was able to hold his granddaughter in his arms for the first time. "I expect we shall be seeing a lot of her," he said to my mother.

On Saturday after lunch, my wife and I went for a walk along the cinder track, past the Finchley Lawn Tennis Club, through the gap in the railings, and over the bridge to the lane leading between the two halves of the Finchley golf course. This was the way I used to go ten years before with my mother, Mrs. Booker, and Mrs. Fransham when we walked the dogs.

On our way back, we met my father. He had come out to meet us, intending to walk back with us. He was standing by the bridge over the stream. We stopped, expecting him to join us, but he looked straight into my eyes and said,

"You go on ahead." I questioned this, but he insisted, so we left him standing there by himself under the chestnut trees by the bridge over the stream. We left for Cornwall that afternoon, and I did not see him again.

On receiving my wings, I volunteered for the Airborne Early Warning role, and joined 849 Squadron at the Royal Naval Air Station, Culdrose, in Cornwall, where I started operational training on the Gannet, an unarmed, cumbersome, turbo-prop aircraft with constant-speeding, co-axial, contra-rotating propellers driven by Double Mamba engines. Management of the engines and propellers was a complex business. If you inadvertently closed the throttles through the flight idle gate with the undercarriage down, the propellers went to fully fine, the aircraft dropped out of the sky like a brick and you had to have thousands of feet and quick reactions to survive. Some didn't.

Quite soon after starting on the Gannet, I realized that in one respect my father had been right, in that I was indeed not much more than a glorified taxi driver for the two observers who operated the radar. But one had to be quite a skilled taxi driver all the same. Gannets were all-weather aircraft and the nature of their work—providing radar cover to detect low-flying aircraft—required them to spend much of their patrol time over the sea below two thousand feet, often in cloud.

On Sunday November 17, 1963, we went to the naval mess at Culdrose to watch the weekly movie show. Afterwards, we returned to our married quarter, paid off the baby sitter, and went to bed—to be awakened in the early hours by the phone ringing. It was the police, informing me that my father had suffered a heart attack and was dangerously ill. We wrapped the baby up, packed hasty bags, and set out on the two hundred mile drive to London, arriving at 67 Brent Way at seven in the morning, where we were greeted by my mother, who broke the news that JG had died a few hours before.

A relationship between father and son does not come to an end on the death of the father. In my case, it continued to develop over the years, and I now feel that I know my father better, and am much closer to him, than I was while he was alive.

26

Soon after getting married, I started writing romantic short stories for women's magazines, none of which were accepted for publication. But, in spite of receiving over forty editorial rejection slips, I persevered and, while serving aboard HMS *Eagle* at Hong Kong, I wrote a travel article about Macao that was accepted by *Blackwood's Magazine*. So started my writing career.

Navy pilots have plenty of spare time, and I used mine to read widely. My heroes were an odd mix that included Maugham, Steinbeck, Hemingway, Wharton, Fitzgerald, Hardy, de Maupassant, Chekhov, Pasternak, Voltaire, Flaubert, Dostoevsky, Nietzsche, and Tolstoy. I dipped into Jung and Freud, and read how-to books on writing, particularly Thomas Uzzell's excellent *The Technique of the Novel*.

The more I read, the more skeptical I became about religion. Maugham's autobiography *The Partial View* prompted me to read Stuart Hampshire's *Spinoza*, which introduced me to the idea of God and Nature being one and the same thing. Flying night patrols from HMS *Eagle* off the east coast of Africa—without a diversion airfield—was not the safest occupation, and I thought quite a lot about death. My prime concern was in staying alive, and it quickly dawned on me that going to Mass on a Sunday or accepting the Lord Jesus as your Savior cuts no ice on the approach to a pitching carrier deck on a dark night. What mattered, what kept me and my observers alive, was my skill as a pilot, my professionalism, my knowledge of aircraft systems, and my physical and mental fitness. Religion did not seem to me to make a contribution to any of these. I began to see it as an unnecessary detraction that eroded one's self-reliance.

I went on playing at being a Catholic for fifteen years. By the end of that time, after a period of mental turmoil, I came to the conclusion that the play-acting had to stop. Quite apart from the fact that I didn't believe in any of the doctrines I had embraced so enthusiastically while serving aboard HMS *Wasperton*, I found the Roman Catholic Church's close association with the IRA, the Mafia, and the corrupt Masonic lodge P2, repulsive, and I knew that to go on attending Mass or receiving the sacraments of confession and communion would be not only hypocritical but psychologically damaging.

So, I cut myself adrift.

I served in the navy for twenty-five years, as a Fleet Air Arm pilot, minesweeper captain, senior pilot of 849 squadron, and first lieutenant of the frigate HMS *Yarmouth*. But as my literary ambition took precedence over my naval career, and my criticism of the leadership of the Royal Navy made me increasingly unpopular with authority, I was shunted into less prestigious appointments, first as an inspector of ships building, later to naval recruiting, and finally to a sinecure on a NATO staff in Portugal, where I spent most of my office hours and spare time writing my novel *The River Running By*. Published in 1981, a year after I left the navy, it was featured as the book of the month on the front cover of *The Bookseller* magazine.

My second novel, *The Raging of the Sea*, was accepted by Diana Athill, my editor at Deutsch, within four days of submission. And, after writing *The Believer*, which is about the beginnings of the Plymouth Brethren in the nineteenth century, a very charming literary agent called Felicity Bryan whisked me onto the books of Curtis Brown with a commission to write an historical novel about the defeat of the Spanish Armada in 1588.

After *Armada* was published, Andy McKillop, my editor at Collins, suggested that I write a book about Dunkirk, and, while researching *The Fighting Spirit*, I retraced the tracks of Guderian's tanks, and learnt more about the horrors of those weeks in 1940 when JG was racing for the coast with a division of German panzers at his heels.

The full force of the tragedy of Dunkirk hit me when I visited the war cemetery at Dover. I had visited several cemeteries during my research trip in Europe, but this one differed from the rest, because someone with great sensitivity and emotional imagination had decided to place the tombstones in pairs to commemorate the fact that so many soldiers had supported each other on the retreat to the beaches of Dunkirk. I walked among them and wept.

At the end of 1990, my marriage broke up, and I got together with, and later married, Susan Keeble, an artist and book illustrator whose paintings I framed and whose star continues in the ascendant. By this time, I had been handsomely commissioned by HarperCollins to write a novel about the Anglo-Argentine relationship and the Falklands War. But then something rather disturbing happened. After I had submitted the typescript of the novel, which I was to call *The Crying of the Wind*, Michael Shaw, my agent at Curtis Brown, gave me an anonymous critique of it, signed "C," that rubbished it, calling it "little more than a soppy love story."

This was a completely misleading description. The novel describes the insidious destruction of an Anglo-Argentine family, the corruption, torture, and assassination that went on in Argentina in the years prior to the Falklands conflict, the criminal activities of the illegal Masonic lodge, Propaganda Due (P2), and events aboard a hospital ship during the Falklands conflict in 1982.

Before writing the novel, I had done extensive research in Argentina. I had stayed at on estancia, and had interviewed a number of people closely connected—and affected—by the Dirty War, including a nursing sister who served aboard a British hospital ship during the Falklands campaign, the leading journalists Andrew Graham-Youll, of the *Buenos Aires Herald*, Jesus Iglesias Rouco, editor of *La Prensa*, and the widow of a university professor in Salta, who had been "disappeared."

Mike Shaw declined to inform me of the identity of "C." Having written episodes for the television spy series *The Sandbaggers*, whose fictional director of MI6 is known by the same code letter, I was able to put two and two together and guess that, because of its content, my book was being actively discouraged, probably by the Ministry of Defence.

For a while, my confidence faltered and I considered withdrawing *The Crying of the Wind* before publication; but it was published in 1992, albeit with minimal publicity, and when the paperback came out the following year it was in exceedingly small print and virtually invisible in bookstores. It was quickly remaindered, and my publishers informed me that they would not be commissioning any more of my work.

I was then tax investigated and falsely accused of defrauding the Inland Revenue of £20,000. I was refused a grant on a house that had no inside bathroom, and all planning applications I submitted to the local council were blocked.

In the space of ten years, I had written six long novels, three of which had been published in the USA and all of which had been well reviewed. Now, my writing career was dead in the water. I was being killed off. As Jeff Arch, the scriptwriter of *Sleepless in Seattle* remarked to me during a screenwriting seminar, "You never know where the bullet comes from."

All the same, I have a pretty good idea. The Royal Navy and The Ministry of Defence wield considerable influence over the publishing industry in Britain. The Secretary to the "D" Notice Committee has access to all novels submitted for publication, and is able to forbid publishers to publish and put pressure on agents not to represent. It would only have taken a phone call from the secretary of the

"D" Notice Committee (Rear Admiral Pulvertaft, with whom I joined the Navy as a cadet in 1954) to jam the brakes on my writing career.

Perhaps I'm wrong about this; I doubt whether anyone will ever know the truth of the matter. But I do know that no agent or publisher has expressed any interest in my work since publication of *The Crying of the Wind* in 1992, and that my most recent novel, *Jannaway's Mutiny*, which I self published with iUniverse in 2005, was misquoted and rubbished by Vice Admiral Sir Louis Le Bailly in the pages of *Naval Review*.

Other authors have been similarly discredited by naval authority. David Tinker's *A Letter from the Falklands* appears to have been deleted from the Amazon list. After publication of his novel *The Gunroom*, published in 1919, about the bullying of midshipmen before the Great War, Charles Morgan was pressurized to withdraw it; Terence Rattigan was harassed by the Admiralty after the stage production of *The Winslow Boy*; and David Divine's *Mutiny at Invergordon* has been effectively suppressed. It seems that the Royal Navy is unable to bear even the slightest criticism of itself; its inner circle of retired admirals is more secretive than your average Masonic lodge. The Royal Navy's literary magazine, *The Naval Review*, is edited by a retired rear admiral, and is available only its officer members, who are not permitted to reveal its contents to non-members or the press.

As things turned out, all was for the best when someone took steps to bring my literary career to an end. Had that not happened, my son might never have given me *Seven Habits of Highly Effective People* by Stephen R. Covey, and I might never have decided to sharpen my intellectual saw by taking a degree in philosophy at the University of Durham.

My three years at university were the most intellectually exciting and stimulating of my life. At long last, I was being trained to think and argue logically, to open my mind, to read closely and intelligently, and to differentiate between rational arguments and those that are merely persuasive.

The course I took (Philosophy, Single Honors) was splendidly wide-ranging, and I was fortunate to be tutored by professors with international reputations, including J.E. Lowe, Patrick FitzPatrick, Geoffrey Scarre, and David Knight. Of these, David Knight's course *Science and Religion in the 19th Century*, which was twice awarded the Templeton Prize, was particularly enlightening, as it led to my turning my back on religion once and for all. When this happened, the burden of religious anxiety I had carried round with me for fifty years fell from my shoulders, and I found intellectual equilibrium.

So … what do I *really* think?

It seems to me that the universe must necessarily be infinite in infinite ways (or dimensions, or aspects) and that if we use the name "God" at all, we can only do so to refer to the infinite "all-that-is." For if God is supposed to be outside Nature, "he" must be separate from something else, and nothing that is said to be separate from another thing can be regarded as infinite.

This contradiction, I contend, is the flaw that runs through absolutist religions, particularly the warring religions of Christianity, Judaism, and Islam. It is the self-contradictory doctrine upon which they wholeheartedly agree, but upon which each relies to reassure its adherents that theirs is the only true faith.

There is currently a fad for belief in "intelligent design" as a pseudo-scientific alternative to Darwinian evolution. It can be easily deflated. If you believe in an infinitely powerful and wise creator who stands apart from the universe, you are presented with a choice. Either you believe in a theistic God who intervenes in human affairs, or you believe in a deistic "intelligent design" God who, having formed the universe out of nothing and issued immutable laws for it to follow, withdraws and leaves it to run on without further intervention. You can't consistently believe in a God who intervenes in human affairs and yet does not intervene. But here's the problem. Theism reduces God to a less than omnipotent creator who has to work miracles to keep his creation running in accordance with his will, while deism reduces God to a less than omniscient architect or designer whose design has resulted in endless generations of human misery.

The contradiction implicit in believing either in an intelligent design God who should intervene but doesn't, or a creator god who shouldn't have to intervene, but does is, I think, particularly fatal for the Christian religion, as belief in intelligent design rules out the need for the miracles of divine incarnation and bodily resurrection that are essential to the Gospel story; while belief in a creator who is careless enough to build into creation original sin, eternal punishment and the need for salvation rules out the possibility of belief that the original design was the product of an omnipotent and omniscient intelligence in the first place.

The problem can be expressed as a logical inference in the form: "If design infinitely intelligent, then no requirement for Divine intervention; and if Divine intervention required, then design not infinitely intelligent."

The only way out of the impasse that seems rational to me is to accept Spinoza's argument, in his philosophical masterpiece *Ethics*, that God and the universe are one and the same thing, that this "God-or-Nature" is its own cause, and that it is infinite in infinite ways. I explain what I mean by this in *Basic Flying Instruction*.

Because I view space-time as being all of a piece and infinite, I can't go along with any theory that the universe "began" in any way. Belief in a cosmological Big Bang that starts everything off is, I think, as absurd as belief in a divine creator, as it prompts infinite regress questions like "What went bang?" and is a supposition based on mathematics which, as Kurt Gödel so elegantly demonstrated, is incomplete. (For an explanation, read Rudy Rucker's *Infinity and the Mind*).

I much prefer the Chinese concept of Qi (Chi), the infinite energy that pervades, empowers, and forms the infinite universe. It is a worldview that has persisted down the ages and in all cultures. The pre-Socratic philosophers Parmenides and Heraclitus, who said respectively that all is one and all is in flux, seem to me to be close to the same view. The Stoics identified Zeus with Nature. Darwin echoed the same thought in his speculations about pangenesis. Faraday speculated that every atom is nothing more than a centre of force within a field of force. Einstein formalized Spinoza's identification of God and Nature in his Special Theory of Relativity, in which he equated energy (E) with matter in motion (mc^2). And the view that the universe is a single, infinite energy field seems to be confirmed by quantum mechanics, as Gary Zukav engagingly explains in *The Dancing Wu Li Masters*.

Unsurprisingly, absolutist religions abhor this view of the universe, as it denies the existence of individual souls, asserting that there is only one infinite Mind, of which our minds are mere temporal modes. This thought renders absurd all threats of eternal punishment and all promises of eternal bliss, and in doing so discredits the authority of priests, pastors, rabbis and mullahs, together with that of the various political systems to which they lend support.

Is there any point to such speculation? I think so, because a significant moral implication can be derived from the proposition that we are all one, in that once I have grasped it, it becomes obvious that to injure others is to injure myself. This is a precept that applies on a universal scale. Only when we have grasped it can we begin to develop the skill of living in peace and harmony with ourselves and the universe.

27

One morning in my final year at Durham, a letter with a Devon postmark arrived. When I opened it, I thought there must have been a mistake, because it was from a firm of lawyers and contained a check for over £16,000—about $30,000. But it was not a mistake. I had been left this money from the estate of the family of Molly Prettyjohn.

Twenty years before, I had purchased three acres of orchard at Cacela Velha in Portugal. I had never had enough money to do anything with that beautiful stretch of land, but with this legacy, I was able to put a mobile home on it, and for five years in succession Suzie and I wintered there. I planted forty trees—olives, almonds, carobs and figs—and we made friends with the local goatherd, whose wife picked the olives and carobs for us, and brought us fresh eggs and olive oil as payment. I kept a little dinghy hauled up on the beach, and on windy afternoons when the tide was high, I used to sail on the lagoon below the old fort.

Every evening before shutting up for the night, I used to walk among my almond and olive trees, listening to the cicadas trilling and the little owls calling, staring up at the stars and wondering at the greatness of the universe and my good fortune at having had such a privileged and exciting part in its existence; and I often reflected that none of this would have been possible had not my father pulled Molly out of the surf at Lanacombe sixty years before.

I've traveled a long way from those days when I used to pray to be a good boy tomorrow, but I still regard myself as the same person who was carried off Miss Murphy's home-made ice rink at Blackwell House, who set fire to the laurel bushes at Beckside Cottage, and who sat on the oak windowsill in the UCS school library reading *Under the Greenwood Tree*. All the same, I have not been afraid to obey my father's directive to "go on ahead," as I believe that it is in no way disloyal of a son to find himself in disagreement with his father's views.

I think about him a lot these days. When I do, I remember so much about him—his kindness, his courage, his optimism, and his blazing honesty—to which I have not done sufficient justice in this book.

I started writing this memoir when I first developed symptoms of motor neuron disease, or ALS. But although I have been advised that I may have only a few years to live, I do not view the prospect of death with dread, as I regard myself as nothing more that a whirl of energy that must, sooner or later, be re-absorbed into the infinite whirlpool. Besides, I have had a full and exciting life, and a measure of the worldly success that my parents decried. But my greatest achievement of all has been to raise my children to be free from the religious anxiety that characterized my early years, and these days I'm happiest when in their company and the company of my six splendid grandchildren, of whom I am so very proud.

© 2007 Charles Gidley Wheeler

978-0-595-43685-9
0-595-43685-4